The I-S[

AIRCRAFT

MICHELIN

(Title page) A Boeing 737-200 of Far East Air Transport.

> **Note:** No single volume – however wide-ranging – can include every historic and contemporary aircraft. If a model which interests you is not here, perhaps it will be included in the next edition.

© I-Spy Limited 1996

ISBN 1 85671 175 7

Michelin Tyre Public Limited Company
Edward Hyde Building, 38 Clarendon Road, Watford, Herts WD1 1SX

MICHELIN and the Michelin Man are Registered Trademarks of Michelin

A CIP record for this title is available from the British Library.

Edited by Neil Curtis. Designed by Richard Garratt.

Compiled by Brian M. Walters.

The Publisher gratefully acknowledges the contribution of Aerospace Publishing Ltd who provided all the photographs bar one in this I-Spy Guide. CFM Shadow courtesy of CFM Metal-Fax Limited.

Colour reproduction by Anglia Colour Ltd.

Printed in Spain by Graficromo SA.

INTRODUCTION

The speed of development in aviation is astonishing. Within a single lifetime, aircraft technology has progressed from the first frail, wood-and-fabric designs, to the supersonic airliners and combat aircraft of today.

Alas, the rapid pace of new developments has often resulted in the loss of historic aircraft which have been broken up for scrap because their significance was not appreciated at the time. Fortunately, an increasing awareness of the importance of keeping a tangible record of aviation history, has encouraged the foundation of a growing number of museums.

It is even more fortunate that keen enthusiasts have managed to restore many old aircraft to flying condition. Visits to such museums as the Shuttleworth Collection and the Imperial War Museum's Duxford collection, can provide an opportunity to see historic aircraft in the air.

Indeed, many hours of enjoyment may be had by visiting the Army Air Corps, Fleet Air Arm, and RAF Museums, while some private collections will also reward the effort to track them down.

The public viewing areas at airports and airfields will enable readers to identify some of the aircraft listed in this *I-Spy Guide to Aircraft*. The Guide has been divided into three sections to help the reader to sort out the many different aircraft types which may be seen. We have endeavoured to avoid pedantry, using accepted terminology rather than precise but little-used titles.

Some aircraft may be identified only as they fly over Britain, while others on the ground at airports and airfields will allow more time to check them against the pictures. No single volume can include every aircraft that can be seen but we have tried to cover a very broad spectrum.

Not all aircraft fit neatly into the Civil, Military, and Historic categories used here. For example, some historic aircraft, such as the DC-3n, resist retirement, while civil versions of the Hercules show that some military aircraft also have airliner counterparts.

Some aircraft featured in this Guide are rare but the keen-eyed reader may have the satisfaction of spotting those that are the sole remaining examples. By contrast, new aircraft under development for airline or military use have not been included because they have yet to enter service.

Boeing 767

Civil Aircraft

Aerospatiale/BAC Concorde

The technical success of the Concorde has been compared to that of placing a person on the Moon, and it remains the only supersonic airliner to ply regularly across the Atlantic. For a variety of reasons – not least the oil crisis of the 1970s which put supersonic operations firmly beyond the possibility of profit – Concorde was never a commercial success.

Indeed, only Air France and British Airways operate Concorde and,

although the Tupolev Tu-144 was the first supersonic transport (SST) to fly, the Russian aircraft did not remain in service for very long. The slender delta wing of Concorde rarely fails to gain admiring glances and, despite its more than twenty years of service, the design has never appeared old-fashioned. Carrying 100 passengers, Concorde has a maximum cruise speed of 1450 mph (2333 km/h).

Agusta A 109A

The Italian-built A 109 first entered service in 1976 as a twin-engined general-purpose helicopter. Although it has been sold in military versions, as well as for police, air ambulance, and customs use, it is also in service with civilian operators in many countries. The A 109 is notable for its sleek appearance, and it was one of the first helicopters to feature a retractable undercarriage.

The A 109 has proved to be a versatile design, carrying up to eight passengers in its executive transport configuration. A recent new application, however, is for mountain rescue services in Switzerland where safety in a harsh environment is important.

Development of the A 109 is by no means over and new derivatives include the single-engined A 119 Koala which has skids in place of the wheel undercarriage. Powered by two Pratt & Whitney 206C engines in place of the original Allison turboshafts, the new A 109 Power has a longer range.

Airbus A300

The Airbus A300 was the world's first 'wide-body' twin-jet. It was built by a group of European planemakers to challenge the American manufacturers that dominated the airliner market. Typically, the A300 seats some 280 passengers and cruises at 553 mph (890 km/h) over a range of 4240 miles (6820 km).

The wide-body Airbuses are assembled in Toulouse from components supplied mainly by aircraft manufacturers from Britain, France, Germany, and Spain. Several versions have been developed including the current A300-600 (*pictured above*) model which has been in production since 1984. This combines some design features of the later A310, including an innovative cockpit operated by a two-person crew.

The Super Airbus Transporter variant of the A300-600 (sometimes known as the Beluga) is easily distinguished by a very large, unpressurized upper fuselage that can carry the components of other Airbus airliners to the assembly lines. The flight deck is below main deck flow level to ease access for cargo.

Airbus A310

Slightly smaller than the A300 from which it is derived, the A310 is a medium/extended-range airliner which normally seats up to 250 passengers. The A310 retains the same fuselage cross-section as the A300 but is shorter and has a new, advanced-technology wing of reduced span. The horizontal tail surface is also smaller than that of the A300 and, in the longer-range version of the A310, fuel is carried in the tail.

The A310 was a pioneer of the concept of long-range services flown by a twin-engined aircraft – something that is accepted as commonplace these days. Fitted with additional centre tanks in the cargo hold, the A310-300 has a range of up to 6080 miles (9800 km).

Airbus A320

The first 'single-aisle' airliner to be built by the European consortium, the A320 has a number of innovative features. The first subsonic commercial airliner with fly-by-wire control, the A320 is also the first to have side-stick controllers instead of the control columns normally used.

The standard version carries up to 179 passengers and has delta-shaped wingtip fences similar to those on later models of the A300 and A310. Carrying a typical load of 150 passengers, the A320 has a range of up to 3490 miles (5615 km).

A stretched version of the A320, which can carry up to 200 passengers, is designated the A321 (*pictured below*), while the shorter-fuselage A319 variant, can carry 120 passengers.

Airbus A330

A further extension to the 'wide-boy' family of Airbus airliners, the twin-engined A330 typically carries 335 passengers, although planned stretched versions will seat up to 379. The A330 is the first Airbus to be offered with a choice of General Electric, Pratt & Whitney, or Rolls-Royce engines. Although this aircraft is much larger than the A320, the cockpit of the A330 is identical to that of the smaller plane, and this allows pilots to obtain common type ratings.

Airbus A340

To gain the maximum benefit of commonality between its designs, Airbus developed the A340 as a long-range transport with four engines instead of the two that power the A330. With the same basic fuselage, an identical wing and tail unit, as well as a similar cockpit, the A340 permits common type ratings with the A330.

The A340, however, is designed to carry more than 300 passengers over a range of 8695 miles (13,990 km), and further developments will see models with an even longer-range capability.

Antonov An-12

Developed from a military transport, the An-12 is a cargo aircraft which has been produced in large numbers. The An-12 has an integral loading ramp in the rear fuselage to enable bulky cargo to be loaded and unloaded more easily. Similar in many respects to the American-built C-130 Hercules, the An-12 is powered by four Ivchenko AI-20K turboprop engines, and its undercarriage permits operations from very basic airstrips.

An-12s have operated as commercial freighters in many countries, and some are based in the United Kingdom where its maximum payload of 44,090 lb (20,000 kg) has proved useful. The aircraft is often used in support of United Nations' relief activities.

Antonov An-24

The An-24 was flown for the first time in 1960 and, since then, over 1000 examples (including such derivatives as the An-26 [*pictured below*] and An-32) have been produced. Powered by two Ivchenko AI-24 turboprop engines, the An-24 is the most widely used airliner in the former Soviet Union. It carries up to fifty passengers over a range of 341 miles (550 km) and has much in common with the Fokker F-27 Friendship.

The An-24 has a high wing and a rugged undercarriage which enable it to be operated from rough airstrips. Used as much to carry cargo as passengers, the An-24 is an occasional visitor to Britain, although the An-32 derivative is rarely seen. The An-32 is easily distinguished, however, because its engines are mounted over the wings instead of below as on the An-24 and An-26.

Antonov An-124 Ruslan

The world champion heavy-lift cargo airliner, the An-124 is the largest aircraft in series production; it is normally operated by a crew of six. Capable of carrying a maximum payload of 330,693 lb (150,000 kg), the An-124 has an upward-hinged nose as well as clamshell rear doors to permit access for large items.

Two British airlines operate An-124s in collaboration with partners in the CIS, and the aircraft are often chartered to carry outsized loads to remote parts of the world. The four Lotarev D-18T turbofans that power the Ruslan are not noted for their reliability but the aircraft is in constant demand for its enormous capacity.

The An-225 (*right, top and bottom*) powered by six engines is even larger than the Ruslan and was originally designed to carry space orbiters and rockets as an external load. At the moment, however, there is only one example in existence and it is unlikely to be seen over Britain.

ATR 42

The first product of a joint venture between France and Italy, the ATR 42 is a twin-turboprop, high-wing airliner that can accommodate fifty passengers. Designed to replace airliners of an earlier generation, such as the Fokker F-27, the ATR 42 features advanced technology, including PW120 engines made by Pratt & Whitney Canada. The latest models feature six-blade propellers.

The ATR 42's improved economics led to substantial orders from around the world, but some airlines wanted a greater capacity so the stretched ATR 72 (*bottom right*)was introduced in 1989. The larger aircraft can accommodate a maximum of seventy-four passengers, and further developments are being considered. Meanwhile, some 500 ATR airliners have been sold.

Avro RJ85

The Avro RJ85 is identical to the BAe 146-200 and is the most popular of a family of four-jet airliners originally conceived in 1973. Easily distinguished by its high wing and underslung engines, the RJ85 (Regional Jet) and others in the earlier 146 series are often to be seen at London City Airport.

Their low noise and ability to operate from relatively short runways make the RJ series ideally suited for services into city centre airports at Stockholm, Florence, and Berlin, as well as London. After a long period when sales were stagnant, the RJ85 secured important orders from leading European airlines such as Swissair, Sabena, and Lufthansa.

BAC One-Eleven

The BAC 111 was designed in the 1960s to be a successor to the Viscount although it did not succeed in matching the latter's total sales of well over 400. Nevertheless it has proved to be a durable twin-jet which is popular with airlines for its reliability and economy. Sometimes less popular with airport neighbours because of its noisy engines, the One-Eleven has been the subject of noise-reduction modifications. It remains a key element in the fleets of some charter airlines.

A few examples serve as executive jets but the largest variant, the 111-500 with its capacity for 119 passengers, is the most sought-after by some airlines. Many examples have found their way to Nigeria where the One-Eleven has become the mainstay of several airlines.

Beech Baron

Thousands of Beech Barons have been built for use as business aircraft, and many are flown by owner/operators who fly themselves when visiting customers. A low-wing aircraft powered by two 300 hp Continental piston engines, the Baron can accommodate up to six people in a comfortable cabin.

At an economical cruising speed of 188 mph (302 km/h), the Baron has a range of 1814 miles (2919 km). For a slight penalty in range, however, the Baron can cruise at 234 mph (376 km/h). In production for over twenty-five years, the Baron has established a firm place for itself in the 'self-drive' business aircraft market.

Beech Bonanza

The Bonanza first appeared many years ago with a 'butterfly' tail (in which the vertical fin was replaced by a V-shaped tail). Since the first model appeared in 1947, however, the great majority of the thousands built have had a conventional tail unit. The family similarity with the Baron is evident from the shape and size of the fuselage which, like the twin, can accommodate six people.

Beech is noted for the quality of its aircraft construction, which accounts for the fact that many Bonanzas are flown by their owners on business. Many others are on the strength of airline flying schools.

Beech King Air

Originally developed as a turboprop-powered version of the twin-piston-engined Queen Air, the King Air also differs from the earlier model in having a pressurized cabin. First entering service in 1964, the King Air had achieved sales of over 1000 within twelve years, and with many more thousands to its credit, derivatives remain in production today.

Although other manufacturers have attempted to produce competitors, the King Air continues to achieve the highest sales for executive aircraft in its class. The Super King Air development is distinguished by its T-tail but the 'Super' prefix is apt to be dropped nowadays. The Model 350 is the latest and largest in the series, accommodating up to twelve passengers and having the longest fuselage. Winglets also distinguish the King Air 350 from earlier models.

Beech King Air C90SE (top) and Super King Air 350 (right)

Beech 1900 Airliner

Owing much to the King Air design, the 1900 has been considerably stretched to accommodate nineteen passengers in a pressurized cabin. As the name indicates, the aircraft has been designed for the regional airline market but several have been sold as executive aircraft, carrying fewer passengers in greater comfort.

The original version of the 1900, which first entered service in 1984, had a fuselage similar in basic design to that of the King Air. Market demand for a 'stand-up' cabin, however, led to the 1900D (*pictured above*) which has a 28.5 per cent increase in volume. This is now the standard model and has a range of 794 miles (1278 km); it cruises at 330 mph (532 km/h).

Beech Starship

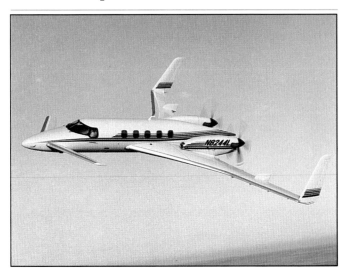

The all-composite Starship entered service as an eight-seat executive aircraft in 1990 but, despite early promise, production has now ended. Powered by two PT6A-67A turboprop engines driving pusher propellers, the Starship looks as if it is flying backwards.

The horizontal 'tail' at the front of the fuselage is not a tail but canards which help to provide pitch axis control, while the wingtip fins – called tipsails – function as rudders. Although a gallant attempt to break away from conventional design, the Starship must be deemed a failure – some say because it is too heavy and complex.

Beech 400A

The Model 400A twin-jet executive aircraft was acquired by Beech from Mitsubishi in 1985 to add a jet to the company's product range. The 'A' version incorporates some improvements over the initial production model, thought necessary for the civil market. A further modification to meet a United States Air Force need for a trainer, however, resulted in an order for over 200 examples.

As a business jet, the 400A can accommodate eight passengers and will fly at 518 mph (834 km/h) over a range of over 2000 miles (3500 km), cruising at a height of 41,000 ft.

Bell 206

The Model 206 JetRanger was originally designed in the early 1960s to meet a US Army need for a light helicopter. It went on to become a classic in its own time and sold in great numbers to military and to civil customers.

Carrying up to three passengers and powered by a single Allison 250-C20 turboshaft, the 206 has proved to be a versatile helicopter suitable for a variety of roles including airborne law enforcement. Developments have included the LongRanger which has an extended fuselage and can carry five passengers. A twin-engined version, called the TwinRanger, is now available.

Bell 222

Although production of the Bell 222 ceased after 184 examples had been produced, its sleek lines led to the Model 230 (*top right*) and the later Model 430
(*bottom right*). Each is similar in appearance and capable of carrying nine passengers. The 222 has a retractable undercarriage and has found applications in
such special roles as law enforcement and medical evacuation.

The latest version cruises at 161 mph (259 km/h) and has a range of 379
miles (609 km). Although the 222 features the twin-blade main rotor typical of
Bell designs, the later models are available with four-blade main rotors which
give a smoother ride.

Originally powered by two Textron Lycoming LTS 101 engines, the Model
230 derivative is powered by Allison 250-C30G2 turboshafts to improve reliability and performance. The later Model 430 incorporates additional improvements and is available with either a wheeled or skid undercarriage.

Boeing 707

Although the de Havilland Comet is rightly credited with being the first jet airliner, it was the Boeing 707, seating up to 189 passengers, that thrust the airlines into the jet age. The design was launched into production as the KC-135A tanker/transport for the United States Air Force in 1954, however, and another year elapsed before PanAm placed an order for twenty airliners.

At the same time, PanAm contracted for a similar number of Douglas DC-8s but it was the 707 that eventually dominated the long-range jet airliner market. Indeed, the four-jet airliner led to the development of a family of designs with the same upper fuselage cross-section. Variants of the 707 included a convertible passenger/cargo model, while the 720 had a shorter fuselage with seating for 149 passengers.

The glory days of the 707 are over, however, and of the few remaining in service, most serve as freighters, operating as the airline equivalent of tramp steamers. The type is becoming quite rare.

Boeing 727

Entering service in 1964, the Boeing 727 trijet became the first jet airliner to achieve sales of more than 1500. Indeed, the 727 came to dominate the short- to medium-range market in much the same way as the 707 achieved most sales in the long-haul arena. Initially produced as a 125-seat airliner, the 727-100 was stretched by 20 feet (6 metres) to become the -200 version with accommodation for a maximum of 189 passengers.

Although the rear-engine configuration made for a very quiet cabin, however, new noise regulations have obliged 727 operators to fit 'hush kits' or even replace the original engines with Rolls-Royce Tays.

Boeing 737

The 'baby' of the Boeing jet airliner family, the 737 has been the most successful numerically, with 1114 of the -200 model produced by 1989. Designed as a short-haul airliner, it was introduced after the BAC One-Eleven and Douglas DC-9 but outsold them both.

Accommodating up to 130 passengers, many 737-200s remain in service but they have been superseded by the -300 (*pictured*), -400, and -500 models. Each of the new models is powered by CFM56 turbofans in place of the original Pratt & Whitney JT8 turbojets. With sales figures for the second generation 737 well into four figures, the design is about to be produced in a third-generation variant, with -600, -700, and -800 models to enter service in the later 1990s.

Boeing 747

PanAm launched the 747 into service in 1970 and it remains the largest passenger airliner in production today. Developed from Boeing studies for a large logistics transport for the United States Air Force (which led to the C-5A), the 747 became a logical successor to the 707.

Some of the early -100 models remain in service (although mostly as freighters) but the 747 has been developed in several versions. The latest is the -400 which is easily distinguished by winglets and an extended upper deck. Other, less obvious improvements in this latest model include a two-crew cockpit and a maximum range of 8450 miles (13,600 km).

The 747SP (*above*) was an unusual variant produced in 1976, featuring a shorter fuselage and an extended range of 6900 miles (11,000 km). All 747 models are to be seen in the UK from time to time.

Boeing 757

The pencil-thin fuselage of the Boeing 757 easily distinguishes this short/ medi-um-range member of the family. It entered service in 1984 and has since estab-lished a strong position in the market. Accommodating up to 239 passengers, the 757 is the first of a new technology family produced by Boeing, although it retains the fuselage cross-section of the earlier 707/727 and 737.

Powered by two Pratt & Whitney PW2040 or Rolls-Royce 535E4 turbo-fans, the 757 has a maximum range of 3247 miles (5226 km) when equipped with the latter.

Boeing 767

Launched as a medium- to long-range airliner in the same year as the A310, the Boeing 767 has outsold its Airbus-built rival. Since entering service in 1982, the 767 has been developed into a number of variants including the stretched -300 which can carry 290 passengers. The basic -200 model normally seats 216 passengers and is widely used throughout the world.

Drawing on the Airbus concept of designing cockpits to permit dual designation for pilots, the 767's controls and instruments are practically identical to those of the smaller 757. Indeed, the handling of the 767 is close enough to the 757 to permit the minimum of training to achieve dual designation.

Boeing 777

At first glance, it is hard to distinguish the 777 from the 767. Both are twin jets and most likely to be seen at the long-haul passenger terminals at British airports. The 777 is very much bigger than the 767, however, carrying up to 400 passengers, although most are configured to seat less.

Intended to meet the needs of airlines that cannot fill the 747 on some long-haul routes, the 777 has won important orders from airlines in the Middle and Far East, as well as in Europe and the United States. The big Boeing twin is unusual in having been permitted to enter service with approval to fly long over-water routes, rather than wait until it established a record of reliability.

British Aerospace ATP

The last design to bear the British Aerospace company name, the ATP (Advanced Turbo Prop) is a radical development of the 748 twin turboprop airliner originally built by Avro in the 1960s. The fuselage stretch to accommodate up to sixty-four passengers in the ATP, however, has substantially changed the appearance of the 748 which originally seated a maximum of fifty-eight.

While the 748 achieved sales of over 300 throughout the world, the ATP totally failed to reach three figures, and an attempt to revitalize the design as the Jetstream 61 was abandoned when Britain's regional airliner manufacturers pooled their resources in a European group called Aero International (Regional). Examples of the 748, ATP, and Jetstream 61 are likely to be seen for many years to come.

BAe 125-800

As the DH 125, this twin-jet executive aircraft first flew in 1962. Since that time, the 125 has become one of the most successful of business jets, and ownership of the design passed to Hawker Siddeley, British Aerospace, and more recently Raytheon.

With sales of over 800 to its credit, the 125 has been the subject of continued refinement, and the -800 version can carry six passengers over a range of 3305 miles (5318 km). The -1000 is a stretched version, however, that can accommodate up to fifteen passengers and has a range of 3961 miles (6375 km). Both variants are now produced in the United States and are sold under the 'Hawker' name.

Demonstrators of the 800 and 1000 are shown flying together (above), with their distinctive liveries reflecting their British origin. The differences between the -800 (top) and the -1000 (bottom) can be seen on the opposite page.

Canadair Regional Jet

Developed from the Challenger executive jet, the Regional Jet has a fuselage stretch to accommodate fifty people in a standard configuration. Although there have been several attempts to produce a small jet airliner, none has enjoyed the success of the Regional Jet.

Airlines in several countries have acquired the Regional Jet which is now a regular visitor to airports in Britain. Carrying a maximum payload, the ER (Extended Range) version of the Regional Jet has a range of 1630 miles (2623 km), and it normally cruises at 529 mph (851 km/h).

In its original executive aircraft form, the Challenger is in service with many corporations around the world carrying a maximum of nineteen passengers – but usually rather less.

CASA C-212

The C-212 was first produced in 1971 to meet a Spanish Air Force requirement for a multi-role transport. Although capable of carrying sixteen paratroops, the C-212 also found a market as a nineteen-seat civil airliner in which guise it achieved sales in several countries including the United States.

The box-like fuselage and rear loading door also enable the C-212 to accommodate bulky cargo. A series of refinements, including a stretched fuselage, led to the current Series 300 which can accommodate up to twenty-six passengers or twenty-four paratroops. The latest version can be distinguished by the 45° dihedral wingtips. In some countries the C-212 is operated as an air ambulance while, in others, it is used on coastal patrol duties.

CASA CN-235

Strictly speaking, this should be referred to as the Airtech CN-235 because it is an international project in which CASA of Spain and ITPN of Indonesia each has an equal holding. While production of components is still shared between the two companies, however, they have tended to go their own way in marketing terms, sometimes competing with one another for the same order.

As a civil airliner, the CN-235 can carry forty-four passengers over a range of 932 miles (1501 km). Although it has a pressurized cabin, however, the CN-235 can also be used to carry freight which can be loaded via a rear ramp/door. A high-wing, twin turboprop design, the CN-235 can be operated from rough airstrips, and has therefore proved popular as a military transport, as well as a regional airliner.

Cessna 150/152

The classic, braced high-wing, single-engined Cessna 150 became the standard two-seat trainer/club aircraft in many countries. It was built in its thousands before evolving into the improved 152. Indeed, a total of 7500 Model 152s had been built by 1986, including some under licence in France.

Bizarre product liability laws in the United States led Cessna to stop production of its light aircraft altogether in 1987, however, so flying clubs and schools have had to make do with increasingly ageing models. It says much for the resilience of the design, that 150s and 152s will be around for many years to come.

Although the law has been changed in the United States, Cessna has no plans to put the 152 back into production.

Cessna 172

The 172 is similar in appearance to the slightly smaller 150/152 but can carry a total of four people. More than 35,000 172s have been built, and no other manufacturer has come close to challenging this remarkable record. Although Cessna stopped production of the 172 in 1987 in the face of crippling insurance claims resulting from product liability laws, these have now been relaxed and production restarted.

Despite the opportunity presented by the years when Cessna ceased production of its light aircraft, no competitor succeeded in filling the void, and already the 'new' 172 is expected to be produced in thousands once more.

Cessna 208 Caravan I

The high braced wing and tricycle undercarriage of the Caravan I are familiar Cessna design features. The 208 is a totally new concept, however, and much bigger than the company's other single-engined aircraft.

Powered by a PT6A turboprop engine, the Caravan I can carry fourteen passengers over 1117 miles (1797 km), although many examples are used to carry freight. Federal Express alone operates over 300 examples, although these will not be seen in the United Kingdom. The Grand Caravan is a stretched model designed to accommodate more cargo, and it is available as a floatplane.

Cessna 310

Production of the 310 began in 1953, and it became an instant success as a twin-engined business aircraft. Seating up to six people, the 310 also served as an air taxi and advanced trainer, although the majority of the several thousand produced were sold for executive transportation.

Key features of the 310 were incorporated in the 340 and other models produced by Cessna, and, although manufacture of twin-piston- and turboprop-powered models was suspended in 1987, many remain in service. At present there are no plans to resume production of the Cessna twin-piston-engined range.

Cessna 337

Known as the Skymaster, the 337 is easily distinguished by its twin-boom lay-out. This permits the installation of two engines on the centre-line of the aircraft – one at the front and the other at the back. This enables pilots more used to han-dling single-engined aircraft to control the 337 without difficulty in the event of a single engine failure, because it would not be inclined to swing.

There are other features which account for the popularity of the 337, how-ever, over 2000 of which were produced. The high wing of the 337 provides bet-ter visibility for the crew than most twins, while its retractable undercarriage helps it to achieve a maximum speed of 206 mph (332 km/h).

The 337 is capable of carrying six people, but has also functioned as a cargo carrier. Mounting rockets and machine guns, it has been used as a ground-attack aircraft in Vietnam and Zimbabwe.

Cessna F406 Caravan II

Cessna became highly skilled in the art of producing variations on twin-engined light aircraft designs, offering the market a wide range of models. Reims Aviation produced over 5000 light singles under licence from Cessna and was a logical partner to collaborate on the development of the twins as well.

The turboprop, unpressurized F406 is a result of this partnership. Carrying up to twelve passengers, the Caravan II light business and utility transport incorporates many features of earlier Cessna designs. It has found a wide range of applications including customs and fishery patrol, as well as a light cargo aircraft for which no less than twenty eight have been acquired by Aviation Lease Holland.

Cessna Citation VII

One of a growing family of business jets, the Citation VII is a prime example of Cessna's ability to develop seemingly endless variations on a basic design. Despite entering the executive jet market after most of its rivals, Cessna quickly established a niche and has produced large numbers, once again achieving four figures.

The straight-winged models were often acquired by companies that wanted to move up to jets from turboprops, but the Citation III was the first to have swept wings (and therefore offer higher speeds). The Citation VII (*pictured*) is a more powerful version of the III and it can carry nine passengers, cruising at 550 mph (885 km/h) over a range of 2533 miles (4077 km).

CFM Shadow

The Shadow has been in continuous production since 1984, to become one of the most successful microlights. Designed to provide low-cost sport flying, the Shadow is available in kit form for home-build construction; the airframe is made from aluminium, wood, and glass fibre.

The Shadow can seat two in tandem, is impossible to stall, and has a minimum flying speed of 25 mph (41 km/h). Cruising at 75 mph (121 km/h), the Shadow has a range of 160 miles (257 km), although the more powerful Streak Shadow has an improved performance and a range of 400 miles (643 km).

Commander 114

The Commander 114B is the latest version of a four-seat, single-engined aircraft derived from the Aero Commander Model 112. First flown in 1970, the Model 112 was produced by North American Rockwell which later refined the design as the Model 114.

Gulfstream Aerospace acquired the design and production rights before disposing of them in 1988 to the Commander Aircraft Company. The present owners have further refined the design of the Model 114 although, dimensionally, it is much the same as the original.

Powered by a 260 hp Lycoming engine, the Model 114 has a retractable undercarriage, cruises at 189 mph (304 km/h), and has a range of 773 miles (1245 km). The aircraft is used for touring, business aviation, and training.

The Commander 114 is shown in the foreground above, with 112B and the 112TC-A behind it to the left and right.

Convair 580

It is a tribute to the sound construction of the original piston-engined Convair 240/340/440 airliners, that they proved to be so suitable for conversion to turboprop power. Widely used as passenger aircraft in the late 1940s and throughout the 1950s, the Convair 240 evolved into a family of short-haul airliners, the biggest of which, the Model 440, could accommodate fifty-two passengers.

The advent of turboprop engines, however, resulted in several proposals to upgrade the Convairs to improve their performance and operating economics. More than 230 examples were subsequently converted, with the Allison 501 proving to be the most popular of the alternative engines.

These permitted a cruising speed of 342 mph (550 km/h), compared to the 300 mph (483 km/h) of the Convair 440. Some remain in service today, those operated as freighters by DHL being the most frequent visitors to Britain.

Dassault Falcon 20

A 'first-generation' business jet, the Falcon 20 entered service in 1965 and quickly penetrated the United States market with a large order from PanAm's Business Jets Division. Seating up to ten passengers, the twin jet Falcon 20 enjoyed considerable success, not only as an executive aircraft but also carrying freight for Federal Express.

Today, the largest operator in the UK is FR Aviation based at Bournemouth airport where a fleet of twenty is used to provide training services for the Royal Navy. Some of these were formerly operated by FedEx (which has graduated to larger aircraft) but they have proved to be adaptable to the new role. Similar in appearance, the smaller Falcon 10, with a standard layout for four to seven passengers, followed the Falcon 20 but neither is in production today.

Dassault Falcon 900

The Falcon 900 is the latest long-range executive jet design from Dassault. Like the earlier Falcon 50 which has the same fuselage cross-section as the Falcon 20, the Falcon 900 is a trijet but it has a much wider cabin. Indeed, the Falcon 900 can accommodate nineteen passengers, compared to a maximum of twelve in the Falcon 50.

Dassault is Europe's only business jet manufacturer and it provides strong competition to the North American companies which would otherwise dominate the market. The Falcon 900 has a maximum cruising speed of 575 mph (927 km/h) and can carry eight passengers over a range of 4491 miles (7227 km).

Employing the same fuselage cross-section as the Falcon 900, the twin-jet Falcon 2000 has been designed as a replacement for the Falcon 20.

*The Dassault Falcon comes in several variants, the 900 (*opposite and in the background above*), the 50 (*above*), and the 2000 (*below*).*

de Havilland Chipmunk

The Chipmunk was originally designed and built in Canada by the then subsidiary of the UK-based de Havilland company. The two-seat basic trainer quickly attracted orders from many air forces, however, including the RAF. So, although production in Canada ended in 1951, it continued for several more years in the United Kingdom.

The Chipmunk is being retired from military service in Britain, but many remain in the hands of private owners and flying clubs. The tandem seating and a tail-wheel undercarriage of the Chipmunk are considered old-fashioned today but the highly aerobatic aircraft has become a popular classic.

de Havilland Twin Otter

The Twin Otter was designed as a short take-off and landing (STOL) transport for operation in the Canadian bush. Its nineteen-seat capacity, however, exactly met the requirements of the burgeoning 'commuter airline' market in the United States.

The Twin Otter became a popular regional airliner although its STOL capability ensured that it also sold widely to 'bush' operators around the world. Normally fitted with a fixed tricycle undercarriage, the Twin Otter can also operate on floats or skis. Although no longer in production, the Twin Otter will be around for many years to come and some are used to operate airline services in Britain.

de Havilland Dash 7

The largest of the STOL transport aircraft designed by de Havilland Canada, the Dash 7 is powered by four PT6A-50 turboprop engines. Accommodating up to fifty-four passengers, the Dash 7 is generally operated into airports with short runways, rather than into rough airstrips like many of the earlier de Havilland designs.

Although no longer in production, examples of the Dash 7 are still in airline service in Britain. Its STOL capability should ensure continued demand for its services wherever runways are too short for less agile airliners.

de Havilland Dash 8

The Dash 8 reflects a subtle change in the direction of de Havilland Canada's design philosophy. The company initially designed single- and twin-engined 'bush' transports, many of which remain in service. Growing demand for commuter or regional airliners, however, encouraged the design of larger and more conventional airliners.

The Dash 8-100, therefore, was designed initially as a thirty-seven-seat airliner. But the growth in air transport led to demands for increased capacity, so the fuselage was stretched to become the fifty-seat Series 300.

Both versions are in airline service in Britain. The Series 100 cruises at 304 mph (491 km/h) and has a range of 944 miles (1519 km). Work has begun on the design of a Series 400 seventy-seat version but this will not enter service until the late 1990s.

de Havilland Dove

The Dove was the first civil transport aircraft to be built in Britain after World War II, but its sleek lines do no look out of place today. Powered by two 380 hp de Havilland Gipsy piston engines, the Dove can carry up to eleven passengers at 288 mph (463 km/h) over ranges up to 500 miles (804 km). Few of the 540 produced remain in service today because most airlines prefer larger, turbine-powered aircraft.

Some remain airworthy, however, operated as executive aircraft. Others have been modified by the installation of more powerful engines, and stretched to accommodate eighteen passengers.

The Dove led to the development of the four-engined Heron which could carry seventeen passengers, while de Havilland's Australian subsidiary produced the three-engined Drover based on the British design.

Douglas DC-6

Dating back to the late 1940s, the DC-6 was the first pressurized airliner to be produced by Douglas. Developed as a successor to the unpressurized DC-4 which was built primarily for military use during World War II, the DC-6 used the same wing but featured a fuselage stretch to accommodate more passengers.

A further stretch resulted in the DC-6B which could carry ninety-two passengers. Although it led to the yet larger DC-7, history has judged the former to be one of the most successful airliners of its time.

Powered by four Pratt & Whitney R-2800 piston radial engines, the DC-6B cruises at 316 mph (509 km/h) and has a range of 3000 miles (4,828 km).

It says much for the DC-6 that, although production ended in 1958, some still remain in airline service, although used mostly to carry cargo.

Douglas DC-8

The DC-8 is similar in appearance to its contemporary, the Boeing 707. Indeed, it was launched in the same way by an order for twenty placed by PanAm in 1955. Although much the same in terms of capacity and performance as the Boeing 707, however, the DC-8 was outsold by its rival.

Some say that Boeing's success lay in its ability to develop many variants of the 707 although the stretched DC-8 Series 60, introduced in the mid-1960s, became the most popular of all the first-generation long-range jet airliners. With a total of 556 of all models produced, the DC-8 was clearly a successful design but the later Series 60 became the most popular with airlines long after production ended.

Indeed, powered by CFM56 turbofans in place of the original Pratt & Whitney JT3 engines, some Series 60 DC-8s were converted to a Series 70 configuration (*pictured above*). Many DC-8s have been converted to carry cargo.

Dornier 228

Introduced in the early 1980s, the first 228s could carry fifteen passengers in an unpressurized cabin. Market demand led to the 228-200 series, however, which has become the standard model. This increased the passenger capacity to nineteen, although some models carry cargo while others are used in a coastal patrol role.

Seen to be a natural successor to the older Twin Otter, the 228 has a high wing of advanced design which permits a STOL performance as well as a maximum cruise speed of 269 mph (434 km/h). For a 'bush' aircraft, the 228 is unusual in having a retractable undercarriage but it can operate from unpaved runways. With a full passenger load, the 228 has a maximum range of 725 miles (1167 km).

Dornier 328

Although the 328 retains the basic wing profile of the 228, it is much larger and can carry thirty-three passengers in its pressurized fuselage. Introduced in the early 1990s when airlines were experiencing a deep recession, the 328 has had to struggle to win orders.

With a maximum cruising speed of 397 mph (639 km/h), however, the 328 retains the STOL capability of its smaller stablemate. Employing an electronic noise-cancellation system, the 328 has a particularly quiet cabin.

Embraer Bandeirante

The first transport aircraft to be designed in Brazil, the Bandeirante is a nineteen-seat, low-wing commuter airliner. Powered by two PT6A turboprop engines, the Bandeirante entered airline service in 1973. It proved to be the right aircraft at the right time and many hundreds were sold around the world – particularly in the United States.

Although series production ended in 1990 with the delivery of the 500th example, small numbers of the Bandeirante have been manufactured since then. Although the majority were delivered to airlines, some have been supplied to air forces. Military versions include a maritime surveillance aircraft as well as light transports.

Embraer Brasilia

Encouraged by its success with the Bandeirante, Embraer designed the thirty-seat Brasilia which entered service in 1985. A conventional low-wing design powered by two Pratt & Whitney PW118 turboprops, the Brasilia has sold in substantial numbers, although not yet matching the total of its smaller brother.

Cruising at 357 mph (574 km/h), the Brasilia is one of the fastest of the regional airliners, and it can carry a full payload 575 miles (926 km). With a fuselage based on that of the Brasilia, Embraer designed a fifty-seat regional jet for service entry in the mid-1990s. An extended range version of the new EMB-145 has a full payload range of 1356 miles (2185 km), cruising at 497 mph (800 km/h).

Enstrom F-28

The F-28 is one of comparatively few piston-engined helicopters in current production. Carrying three people including the pilot, the F-28 is used for a wide range of tasks including training and crop spraying. Most helicopter operators have switched to turbine-powered models, however, and in response to this demand, Enstrom developed the Model 480 which can carry four people.

The F-28 cruises at 112 mph (180 km/h) but a developed model – the F-280FX – is slightly faster and, at 300 miles (483 km), has a longer range. Some Enstrom helicopters are operated in Britain, mostly by private owners.

Eurocopter BO-105

Originally developed in Germany by MBB, the BO-105 is now among the range of products manufactured by Eurocopter. Formed by combining the helicopter divisions of Aerospatiale and MBB, Eurocopter is a world-class manufacturer that offers strong competition to the major North American companies.

The twin turbine BO-105 first flew in 1967, and it has become a popular model, with production well into four figures. Carrying up to five people, the BO-105 is a versatile helicopter much used by police and air-ambulance operators.

Clam-shell doors at the rear of the fuselage aid the loading of strctchers but, in military use, the BO-105 can carry anti-tank missiles or other weapons. The BO-105 has a range of 345 miles (555 km) and cruises at 150 mph (242 km).

Eurocopter Twin Squirrel

The Twin Squirrel is a twin-engined version of a light helicopter originally developed by Aerospatiale as a successor to the Gazelle. Known as the Ecureuil in France and as the A-Star in America, the Squirrel and Twin Squirrel have sold in substantial numbers in civil and in military markets.

In Britain, the Twin Squirrel has become the preferred helicopter with police air wings, and many constabularies have selected one of several variants. Fitted with loudspeakers, a searchlight, TV, and forward-looking infra red (FLIR) cameras, the Twin Squirrel has become a valuable aid to police work.

The Twin Squirrel can carry heavier loads than its single-engined counterpart and it has a range of 448 miles (722 km), cruising at 140 mph (225 km/h).

Eurocopter BK-117

Developed by MBB in collaboration with Kawasaki, the BK-117 is now part of the Eurocopter range which brought together the product lines of the French and German partners. It is available with a choice of LTS 101 or Arriel engines.

Bearing some resemblance to the BO-105, the influence of the German design is evident. Indeed, some BO-105 components are interchangeable with those of the larger BK-117. A multi-purpose helicopter, the BK-117 can carry up to nine passengers in addition to the pilot, although it is usually configured to accommodate rather less.

Widely used in the United States as an air ambulance, the BK-117 has found a new role in Britain where fire brigades have found it useful for carrying special equipment to the scene of a major fire. The concept of avoiding delays caused by traffic jams, is leading to growing interest in the BK-117 which has the right cabin size to accommodate firemen and equipment.

Eurocopter Dauphin

The twin-turbine-powered Dauphin has been the subject of continuous development since it first appeared in 1972 as a ten-seat, medium-sized helicopter. It
was then fitted with a fixed main/tail-wheel undercarriage and was powered by
a single engine.

In the ensuing years, the helicopter has changed substantially although the
tail rotor still takes the form of a 'fenestron' – a ducted fan in the tail. Now fitted with a retractable tricycle undercarriage, the Dauphin is powered by two
Turbomeca Arriel engines.

Used by civil operators for such tasks as servicing offshore oil rigs and carrying patients, the Dauphin has also been supplied to army, navy, and air force
users. It is known as the Panther in its military guise.

Eurocopter Puma

Development of the Puma began in the mid-1960s in response to a French Army requirement for a medium-sized helicopter. It became part of a co-production deal between France and Britain, and the basic model was acquired by the RAF as well as by the French Army.

The Puma was quickly seen to have a potential as an offshore oil rig support helicopter, however, and of the large numbers sold to civilian operators, many are employed for such tasks.

Variously known as the Cougar, Super Puma, and Tiger, developments of the basic model meet a variety of civil and military requirements. The passenger capacity of the original model has increased from sixteen to twenty-four. The Puma has been licence produced in several countries, including South Africa where it is known as the Oryx.

Eurocopter EC-135

The first fruit of collaboration between the two parent companies which formed Eurocopter, the EC-135 began life as the BO-108; it was seen to be a successor to the BO-105. With technical inputs from the French partner, however, the BO-108 was refined by the substitution of a fenestron for the original tail rotor.

This helps the EC-135 to achieve low noise levels, as well as a top speed of 178 mph (287 km/h), and carry up to seven people. No longer posing competition to the French helicopters that now form part of the Eurocopter range, the EC-135 is seen to be Europe's answer to the new Explorer produced by McDonnell Douglas.

Extra 300

Produced in Germany, the Extra 300 is a tandem-seat aerobatic aircraft powered by a 300 Lycoming piston engine. It is expensive to own and fly an aerobatic aircraft, so some Extras are sponsored by major companies to function as 'flying billboards' at air shows.

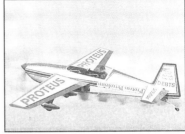

The Extra 300 has a rate of climb of 3300 feet (1005 m) per minute and is stressed to plus or minus 10g. That is ten times normal gravity weight and very much more than the modest limits that could be tolerated by a Cessna 152, for example. The maximum level speed of 213 mph (343 km/h) is also considerably more than could be achieved by a conventional light aircraft.

Fairchild Metro

The long thin fuselage of the Metro has been a familiar sight at American airports since the 1970s but it is only in recent years that examples have entered service in Europe. The Metro is a nineteen-seat commuter airliner with a pressurized cabin. It is powered by two Garrett TPE 331 turboprop engines, and has been produced in substantial numbers

The Metro 23 is the current model which cruises at 331 mph (534 km/h) and has a range of 900 miles (1450 km) carrying a full passenger load. Some variants, known as the Expediter, are operated in an all-cargo configuration.

Fokker 50

Designed to succeed the highly successful F27 Friendship, the Fokker 50 is a high-wing, fifty-seat airliner powered by two Pratt & Whitney PW 125 engines driving six-blade propellers. Although seemingly identical to the F27, in fact more than 80 per cent of the component parts are new or modified compared to the earlier design.

Powered by Rolls-Royce Dart engines, many hundreds of the Friendship airliners remain in service, and some are to be seen at UK airports. The high-pitched whistle distinguishes the F27 from the rather quieter Fokker 50.

Carrying a full passenger load, the Fokker 50 has a range of 1400 miles (2253 km) cruising at 325 mph (522 km/h).

Fokker 100

The Fokker 100 twin jet was announced in 1983, as follow-on development of the F28 twin jet which had been in production since 1964. While the largest F28 could accommodate eighty-five passengers, however, the Fokker 100 entered airline service in 1988 with a capacity for 107.

Powered by two Rolls-Royce Tay engines, the Fokker 100 has a maximum range of 1969 miles (3167 km), cruising at 528 mph (850 km/h). Although significant orders were placed by some United States' airlines, Fokker was pressed to develop a smaller version with a reduced capacity. The result was the Fokker 70 which bears a close resemblance to the original F28!

The F100 (main picture), was a development of the F28 (right), with the F70 (above right) built for reduced capacity.

Grob 115

A two-seat light aircraft, the Grob 115 is of all-composite construction. A low-wing design with a fixed tricycle undercarriage, the G 115 has grown in popularity since it was introduced in 1987. Production was temporarily stopped in 1991, however, and a complete redesign undertaken to enable the company to compete for a USAF trainer competition.

In the event, the task could not be completed in time but the work has resulted in an improved aircraft which is one of the few European designs able to compete in world markets. The G 115 has g limits of +4.4/-1.76 and can perform standard aerobatics. The most powerful version of the G 115 has a maximum speed of 155 mph (250 km/h) and has a range of 453 miles (730 km).

Gulfstream IV

The Gulfstream IV is the latest in a long line of executive jets which sprang from a turboprop aircraft originally designed by Grumman. The Gulfstream V, however, with a range of 6500 miles (10,485 km) will become increasingly evident in the late 1990s when deliveries of this further development get under way.

Easily distinguished from earlier twin-jet Gulfstreams by its winglets, the GIV can carry up to nineteen passengers but is more usually configured to carry rather fewer in greater comfort. A 'flying boardroom', the GIV is widely regarded as the Rolls-Royce of business jets – which is appropriate as it is powered by two Rolls-Royce Tay turbofans.

Handley Page Herald

Formerly known as the 'Dart Herald' because it was developed from an aircraft originally powered by four piston engines, this airliner can carry fifty-six passengers in its Series 200 form. Of the few that remain in airline service, however, most are used to carry freight.

A product of the 1950s, the Herald was designed for the same sector of the market which was tackled more successfully by the Avro 748 and the Fokker F27. Like these similarly sized airliners, the Herald is powered by two Rolls-Dart turboprop engines.

With a maximum cruising speed of 274 mph (441 km/h), the Herald can carry a full payload to a range of 1110 miles (1786 km). Although the Herald has a high wing like the F27, it can be distinguished from its Dutch counterpart by its less pointed nose.

Ilyushin Il-18

Introduced into service with Aeroflot in 1959, the Il-18 became one of the most widely used of transport aircraft in the Former Soviet Union (FSU). Powered by four turboprop engines, the Il-18 can carry up to 110 passengers in high-density seating but few remain in service in this role today.

In common with its western counterpart, the Bristol Britannia, the Il-18 is mostly used to carry cargo nowadays. It can carry its maximum payload over a range of 2300 miles (3700 km), cruising at 419 mph (675 km).

Although the majority of the 800-plus examples produced are operated in the FSU, some were exported to various parts of the world and a few remain in service.

Ilyushin Il-62

The Il-62 was the first four-jet airliner to be designed in the Former Soviet Union (FSU) and it bears a superficial resemblance to the Vickers VC-10 which preceded it by several years. While the VC-10 has now retired from airline duties (to find a new role as a military tanker), however, the Il-62 remains in service with several airlines. Nevertheless, most eastern European airlines have taken the opportunity to replace their Il-62s with western-built aircraft, although Aeroflot still has a fleet of 26 Il-62Ms.

Carrying up to 174 passengers, the Il-62M has a range of 4846 miles (7800 km) cruising at 560 mph (900 km/h).

Ilyushin Il-76

Designed as a replacement for the Antonov An-12, the Il-76 is a high-wing, four-jet, heavy transport aircraft which has proved to be a versatile and durable design. Over 700 Il-76s have been built, and a stretched version has been developed recently.

Although most Il-76s have been produced to meet military needs, Aeroflot operates eighteen, while examples have found their way into service with some western airlines. Carrying cargo weighing up to 110,230 lb (50,000 kg), the Il-76 is often used in support of United Nations' aid activities. With a full payload, the Il-76 has a range of 4535 miles (7300 km).

Ilyushin Il-86

The first wide-body airliner to be designed in the Former Soviet Union (FSU), the Il-86 was developed for its national airline, Aeroflot. The 350-seat Il-86 entered service in 1980 and today the Aeroflot fleet stands at eighteen. Unusual features include integral airstairs which lead passengers into a compartment where they can deposit hand baggage before climbing into the cabin above.

Although as comfortable as any western airliner, the Il-86 has a range of only 1550 miles (2500 km). Performance deficiencies have been ascribed to its Kuznetsov NK-86 engines. The Il-86 has clearly influenced the design of the Il-96 which has new engines to overcome the former's deficiencies. As well as using Russian-built Soloviev PS-90A engines, however, the Il-96 is being produced with Pratt & Whitney PW2037s which give a range of 7330 miles (11,800 km).

Jetstream 31

The Jetstream 31 began life as a Handley Page design in the late 1960s. Development difficulties led to the demise of the company, however, and production was taken over by Scottish Aviation. This company was absorbed into British Aerospace which later spun off Jetstream as a separate company that is now part of the AI(R) group!

The nineteen-seat Jetstream 31 became the most successful airliner in its class, and many are in service in the United States. No longer in production, the J31 will nevertheless remain in service for many years to come. Powered by two Garrett TPE 331 turboprop engines, the J31 has a range of 805 miles (1296 km) cruising at 304 mph (489 km).

Jetstream 41

Only the long fuselage of the Jetstream 41 hints that this is a development from the J31. In most other respects, this twenty-nine-seat airliner differs in appearance from its smaller brother which it has superseded on the production lines at Prestwick.

Regional airlines have tended to grow out of the widely used nineteen-seat J31 into larger aircraft, which is why production is now centred on the J41.

Cruising at 336 mph (541 km/h), the J41 has a range of 679 miles (1093 km). It is now part of the AI(R) product range which has brought together Avro, Jetstream, and ATR into a single group.

Learjet 60

The Learjet 60 is the largest in a range of aircraft that began in 1964 when the Learjet 23 entered service. Employing a wing designed for the P16 Swiss fighter, the Learjet 23 pioneered the business jet concept but was perceived to be too small.

Consequently, while retaining the same basic layout of a swept low wing and two engines mounted on the rear fuselage, the Learjet has grown from a six- to a nine-seater. In the process, however, it has also grown from a small, cramped cabin to one that offers much higher standards of comfort.

Introduced into service in 1992, the Learjet 60 can cruise at 51,000 ft, at 533 mph (858 km). Now part of the Bombardier group (which also owns de Havilland and Canadair), Learjet has developed the Model 45 which will enter service in the late 1990s.

Lockheed Electra

The only large US airliner to be powered by turboprop engines, the Electra was a contemporary of the Vickers Vanguard. Although the Electra outsold its British rival, however, only 170 had been built when production ended in 1962. First deliveries took place in 1959 but, by the mid-1970s, the Electra had been withdrawn from front-line service, as the jet era opened.

Most Electras have been retired but some remain in service as freighters which may be seen in Britain. Conversion from a 100-seat airliner to an all-cargo aircraft involves the installation of a large door in the fuselage ahead of the wing.

The Electra formed the basis for the highly successful P-3 Orion maritime patrol aircraft.

Lockheed TriStar

The L-1011 TriStar marked Lockheed's return to airliner manufacture since the Electra. A trijet powered by Rolls-Royce RB211 turbofans, the TriStar almost brought about the demise of its manufacturer in the wake of the early problems with the engine.

Development of the RB211 bankrupted Rolls-Royce but the TriStar survived, and first deliveries were made in 1972. A 345-passenger wide-body airliner, the TriStar met a market need for a large airliner that was not quite as big as the Boeing 747.

The three-engined McDonnell Douglas DC-10 proved to be a more enduring competitor but, although production of the L-1011 ended after 250 had been built, many remain in service. Some have been converted into tanker/transports for the RAF.

McDonnell Douglas MD-83

The MD-83 is an extended-range version of the MD-80 series, a development of the DC-9 twin jet that first flew in 1965. Indeed, the first MD-80 was known as the Super 80 version of the DC-9 which had undergone extensive development since the Series 10 entered service with a maximum capacity for ninety passengers.

The MD-81 could carry 172 passengers, achieved by stretching the fuselage and fitting more powerful engines. The 3920-mile (6308-km) range of the MD-83 was by no means the last improvement made to the basic DC-9. With sales well into four figures, the MD-90 is a yet further major development.

Powered by IAE V2500 engines in place of the Pratt & Whitney JT8D series, the MD-90 series includes a model that can carry 180 passengers – twice as many as the first DC-9!

McDonnell Douglas MD-11

A trijet clearly derived from the earlier DC-10, the MD-11 can be distinguished by its winglets above and below each wingtip. The DC-10 was originally developed as a Jumbo trijet with a capacity for a maximum of 380 passengers, and many of these remain in airline service.

To win the maximum number of orders in a highly competitive market, several different versions were developed. The MD-11, however, represents a new-generation airliner which incorporates numerous refinements including a 'two-crew' cockpit of advanced design. The MD-11 has a top cruising speed of 579 mph (932 km/h) and can carry a full payload over a maximum of 5760 miles (9270 km).

Many DC-10s retired from passenger service have been converted to carry cargo.

McDonnell Douglas Model 500

Beginning life as the Hughes 500 designed to meet a US Army requirement for a light observation helicopter, the Model 500 first flew in 1963. Since then some 4000 have been built for civil and for military users. Powered by a single Allison 250 C20 turboshaft, the Model 500 can carry six people including the pilot.

Among the several variants produced over the years, the most notable are the MD 520N and MD 530N, easily distinguished by the absence of a tail rotor. Instead, these models have a thicker tail boom in which anti-torque and steering control is provided by air thrust through Coanda slots and steering louvres.

McDonnell Douglas MD 900 Explorer

The Explorer is the first helicopter to be designed by the company from the outset with its NOTAR (no tail rotor) system. (The MD 520N applied the system to an existing design.) Introduced in 1995, the Explorer can carry six passengers and two pilots, and has a maximum speed of 200 mph (321 km/h).

Powered by two engines, the Explorer is notably quieter than earlier helicopters, and the company expects to sell 1000 examples in the first ten years of production. Police operators are among the first customers for the Explorer, and a military version has been developed.

Mil Mi-8

It is said that more than 10,000 Mi-8 (and its Mi-17 and Mi-171 derivatives) have been built. The first prototype flew in 1961 and the Mi-8 has become the standard medium-sized helicopter in the Former Soviet Union (FSU). Indeed, many have been exported around the world and some examples are sometimes to be seen in Britain.

Normally carrying up to twenty-eight passengers, the Mi-8 can alternatively accommodate twelve stretchers, while clam-shell rear doors also permit bulky cargo to be loaded. The Mi-8 has been supplied in large numbers to civil and to military operators. The commercial version has square windows while the military model has smaller circular windows.

Mil Mi-26

The Mi-26 is the largest production helicopter in the world. Most of those produced have been supplied to military operators. The fuselage of the Mi-26 is roughly the same size as that of the C-130 Hercules transport aircraft. Since the end of the Cold War, however, some Mi-26s have found commercial applications and some have supported United Nations' activities in various parts of the world.

The Mi-26 can carry a maximum payload of 44,090 lb (20,000 kg) and its maximum level speed is 183 mph (295 km/h).

Mooney 201

More than 2000 Mooney 201s have been produced, and this four-seat tourer has become a classic among light aircraft. A low-wing design with a retractable undercarriage, the Mooney is easily distinguished by its swept-forward tail. This distinctive feature was introduced by the original Mooney Mite in 1948 and has been retained ever since. Originally a single-seat aircraft, the Mite led to a four-seat version that first appeared in 1953 and has been refined over the years.

The 201 is the current standard model. Cruising at a maximum of 252 mph (406 km/h), the 201 has an endurance of 5 hours 48 minutes. A stretched variant – the 257TLS – was introduced in 1989 to provide a higher standard of comfort.

Piaggio P.180 Avanti

The Avanti first flew in 1986 and is a new-generation executive aircraft. The Avanti can seat up to nine passengers and, although of conventional metal construction, the design is far from conventional. It has straight wings mounted towards the rear of the circular-section fuselage, a T-tail, and foreplanes on the nose.

The wing and two PT6A pusher turboprop engines are at the rear of the cabin so that noise is reduced and there is room to stand up.

The Avanti has a maximum range of 1980 miles (3187 km) and cruises at 299 mph (482 km/h). The unusual appearance of this Italian aircraft makes it easy to identify.

Pilatus PC-12

The PC-12 is the latest product of a Swiss manufacturer which has produced several successful single-turboprop designs. A low-wing aircraft that can seat up to nine passengers, the PC-12 has a pressurized fuselage to enable it to cruise at 25,000 ft.

A versatile aircraft, the PC-12 can carry cargo or stretcher cases instead of passengers, while other variants can be used for border or maritime patrol. The PC-12 is one of a new generation of single-turboprop powered aircraft which perform tasks previously allocated to twin-engined models.

Such is the confidence in the reliability of the PT6A turboprop, however, that several manufacturers have produced transport aircraft powered by this engine. The PC-12 cruises at 309 mph (497 km/h) and has a range of 1842 miles (2965 km).

Piper Cub

The Cub was first introduced in 1930 by the Taylor Aircraft Company. Seven years later the company became Piper Aircraft, and by 1941, 10,000 Cubs had been produced. A two-seat, high-wing design, the Cub has a tail-wheel under-carriage, and the aircraft is notable for its ability to fly into and out of short airstrips.

By 1950, the Super Cub (*pictured above*) was developed with a choice of more powerful engines, although the dimensions differed little from the Cub. Originally powered by a 65 hp Continental engine, the later Cub variants included a 135 hp model. Some Cubs and Super Cubs remain in service, mostly in the hands of private owners. The most powerful Super Cub has a maximum speed of 127 mph (204 km/h).

Piper Warrior

The Warrior is one of many variants of the Cherokee that Piper introduced in 1961. It quickly became popular and more than 30,000 have been built in various models. Although the early Cherokee could seat only two people, most subsequent developments can accommodate four.

The Cherokee Six could seat up to seven people, however, although the Warrior III currently produced, is a four-seater intended mainly for use as a trainer. With the exception of the Cherokee Arrow, which has a retractable undercarriage, all models have a fixed tricycle landing gear. The Warrior III cruises at 145 mph (233 km/h) and has a range of 737 miles (1186 km).

Piper Aztec

The Aztec was developed from Piper's first twin-engined design, the Apache, which entered production in 1954. A four- to five-seat business aircraft, examples of the Apache are still to be seen today and some serve as training aircraft for the airline pilots of tomorrow.

The Aztec grew to become a six-seat executive transport which became popular with air taxi operators because of its useful range of 1310 miles (2108 km). With business travellers preferring the speed and comfort of turboprop or jet aircraft, however, the piston-engined Aztec has been largely relegated to the owner/pilot category of executive aircraft.

Piper Seneca

Essentially a twin-engined version of the Cherokee Six, the Seneca first flew in 1970. The rear fuselage, cabin, and tail of the Seneca are almost identical to that of the single-engined Cherokee Six but the wing has been redesigned to accommodate two 200 hp Continental engines.

The Seneca can accommodate up to six people (including the pilot) but is also widely used by commercial flying schools as a multi-crew and instrument trainer. Over 4000 examples have been built, and the Seneca IV is the latest version which can cruise at 222 mph (9357 km/h).

Under an agreement with Piper, the Seneca II has been produced in Poland by PZL Mielec as the Mewa. Employed as an air ambulance and general transport aircraft, the Mewa is powered by Polish-built Franklin engines.

Piper Navajo

The first Navajo was produced in 1964 as an addition to the Piper range of twin-engined business aircraft. The ability of the Navajo to accommodate up to eight people, however, encouraged its use by air taxi operators as well as by regional airlines.

A fuselage stretch, developed in 1972, resulted in the Navajo Chieftain which superseded the basic model as a ten-seat commuter/cargo airliner. The Chieftain has a range of 1266 miles (2038 km) cruising at 236 mph (380 km/h).

The versatility of this aircraft led to orders from many parts of the world but the substitution of PT6A turboprops for the original Lycoming piston engines resulted in the Cheyenne IA which could carry four passengers in pressurized comfort.

Piper Cheyenne III

Although bearing the same name as an aircraft that was a direct descendant of the Navajo, the Cheyenne III has a lengthened fuselage, increased wingspan, and a T-tail.

First flown in 1979, the Cheyenne III can seat up to nine passengers in a comfortable cabin although, in a high-density airline configuration, it can seat eleven.

The Cheyenne IIIA became the standard model which can cruise at 351 mph (565 km/h) and has a maximum range of 2614 miles (4207 km). The aircraft can cruise at heights up to 35,000 ft – well into the levels at which airliners operate. Perhaps this is why the Cheyenne IIIA has become a popular advanced trainer with airlines in many parts of the world.

Pitts S-2A

The Pitts Special was designed as a single-seat aerobatic biplane in the mid-1940s. The design was subsequently acquired by Christen Industries in 1983, by which time the basic aircraft had been developed into several versions including the two-seat S-2A (*pictured above*).

With a wing span of only 20 ft (6.10 m) and a fuselage length of 17 ft 9 in (5.79 m), the Pitts S-2A became the favourite mount for many aerobatic pilots around the world. Indeed, a number of formation aerobatic teams chose to use the S-2A because it can provide a sprightly display in a relatively small piece of sky

The S-2A can climb at the rate of 1900 ft/min (589 m/min) and it has a top speed of 157 mph (253 km/h), the small size of the aircraft adding to the illusion of higher speeds.

Robinson R-22

The two-seat R-22 is the closest yet to a 'motorcar in the sky'. Introduced in 1979, the R-22 is certainly the most widely used of privately owned light helicopters, and over 2000 have been produced to date.

Some have found use as police helicopters, however, while others are used by commercial flying schools for training. Powered by a single 160 hp Textron Lycoming piston engine, the R-22 has a maximum speed of 112 mph (180 km/h) and a range of 368 miles (592 km).

A demand for a slightly bigger version, capable of carrying four people, led to the development of the R-44. This has a more powerful 260 hp engine derated to 225 hp, and the R-44 cruises at 130 mph (209 km/h).

Rutan VariEze

Burt Rutan is a master in the use of composite materials for the construction of unusual aircraft such as the VariEze. It is a high-performance, two-seater with a canard configuration. Its swept wing and its 100 hp Continental piston engine are mounted at the rear, giving the impression that the aircraft is flying backwards.

Another curious feature is the undercarriage which has fixed main wheels but a retractable nosewheel; this helps the VariEze achieve the remarkably high maximum cruising speed of 195 mph (313 km/h). The 700 mile (1126 km) range is just as remarkable, although, with only one on board, the larger and more powerful Long-EZ (*below*) has a range of 2010 miles (3235 km)!

Saab 340

Originally a joint venture between Saab and Fairchild, the 340 entered service in 1984. By then Saab had assumed control of the programme, and production has been centred in Sweden.

Accommodating up to thirty-seven passengers, the 340 is a low-wing regional airliner powered by two General Electric CT7 turboprops. Carrying thirty passengers, the Saab 340 has a range of 1261 miles (2030 km) cruising at 325 mph (522 km/h).

In the highly competitive regional airliner market, the Saab 340 has sold well throughout the world. The 340B is the current version which is fitted with more powerful engines to improve performance, especially in hot countries.

Saab 2000

Using the same fuselage cross-section as the Saab 340, the 2000 has been designed as a new-generation turboprop. Using two Allison GMA 2100A engines driving 6-bladed propellers, the Saab 2000 narrows the performance gap between this class and jet airliners. The stretched fuselage of the Saab 2000 can carry fifty-three passengers at a speed of 434 mph (700 km/h) over a range of 1179 miles (1900 km).

To achieve low cabin noise levels, a sound-cancelling system has been developed, employing microphones that generate sound at wavelengths which 'defeat' those produced by the engines and propellers.

Saab 2000s flown by Crossair are fitted with a Headup Display (HUD) in the cockpit to enable the aircraft to be landed safely in poor weather conditions.

Shorts Belfast

Only ten Belfast freighters were built in the 1960s and all were originally operated by the RAF. Powered by four Rolls-Royce Tyne turboprop engines, the Belfast made use of the wing designed for the Bristol Britannia airliner. To ease the loading of heavy items through the large rear door, however, the Belfast's wings are high mounted so that the fuselage can be close to the ground.

The victim of defence cuts, the RAF had to dispose of its fleet in 1976, and HeavyLift Cargo Airlines purchased several of them for civil use. It proved to be a wise buy because the Belfast is often in demand to carry large loads that cannot get into such freighters as the Hercules.

Shorts 360

In 1963, Shorts produced the Skyvan, a high-wing aircraft with a box-like fuselage. Almost twenty years later, the company flew its ultimate development in the form of the 360. While the fuselage of the Skyvan was intended to accommodate freight when it was not carrying up to nineteen passengers, however, its derivatives were intended to carry only passengers.

The Shorts 330 (*below*) was the first development, and this retained the twin-rudder configuration of the Skyvan. With its single fin and rudder, however, the 360 was stretched still further to accommodate thirty-six passengers, and some of these unpressurized airliners remain in service.

Curiously, the Skyvan concept has come full circle and some 360s are now being converted into freighters for the United States Air Force.

SIAI Marchetti SF 260

The SF 260 flew for the first time in 1964 and is one of many Stelio Frati designs noted for their fine lines.

A low-wing, single-engined aircraft with a retractable undercarriage, the SF 260 was first produced as an aerobatic trainer and sports plane. The sprightly performance of the SF 260 soon attracted military orders, however, and examples have been delivered to twenty-four air forces around the world. Indeed, more than 800 SF 260s have been produced although, in recent years, demand has fallen as more advanced designs have appeared.

Normally powered by a 260 hp Textron Lycoming piston engine, the SF 260 has also been fitted with the Allison 250-B-17D turboprop.

Sikorsky S-76

The S-76 entered service in 1979 and has since been produced in a number of versions. The various models are almost identical in appearance, however, differing only in the types of engine used.

Accommodating up to twelve passengers, the S-76 is widely used as an executive transport, although many are also employed in carrying personnel to offshore oil rigs. The S-76 is in use as an air ambulance in several countries but, although military versions have been developed, the majority of sales remains in the civil sector.

Its normal cruising speed is 166 mph (269 km/h) and the latest model has a maximum range of 494 miles (798 km).

Slingsby T67 Firefly

The current T67 is a conventional low-wing, two-seat light trainer design but is of all-composite material construction. The earlier all-wood T67A model was a licence-produced version of the Fournier RF-6B originally designed in France.

The aircraft has been considerably developed since production began in the early 1980s – not least the switch to GRP instead of wood. Engine power has steadily increased over the years, growing from 116 hp on the T67B to 200 hp on the T67M200 – a military variant.

The RAF and USAF are among the air forces that use the T67 for basic training but the aircraft has also been chosen to equip many commercial flying schools.

SOCATA TB-10

The TB-10 introduced in 1977 was the first in a series of all-metal light aircraft designed to challenge American dominance of the market.

A low-wing, all-metal four/five seater with a fixed undercarriage, the TB-10 is powered by a 180 hp Textron Lycoming piston engine. The TB-9 (*below*) is similar in appearance but powered by a 116 hp engine, while the more powerful TB-20 and TB-21 have retractable landing gears. The series has proved popular with commercial flying schools and sales have been achieved in the United States – home of the light plane.

The TB-10 cruises at 146 mph (235 km/h) and has a range of 752 miles (1210 km). Over 1000 TB series aircraft have been produced.

Tupolev Tu-134

The Tu-134 was developed in the Former Soviet Union (FSU) at about the same time that the Caravelle, One-Eleven, and DC-9 were being produced in the West.

Like its Western contemporaries, the Tu-134 is a low-wing, T-tailed design with two engines mounted on the rear fuselage. The tough, wide-track undercarriage of the Tu-134, however, enables it to be operated from rough airstrips – a requirement of Aeroflot which was equipped with several hundred. Widely exported to allies of the FSU, some Tu-134s remain in service but they are rapidly being replaced by more recent airliners.

The Tu-134 has a maximum cruising speed of 559 mph (900 km/h) and a range of 1490 miles (2400 km).

Tupolev Tu-154

Produced since 1968, the Tu-154 is a direct counterpart to the Boeing 727 and Trident airliners then being built in the West. A trijet like the Western models, the Tu-154 also has a T-tail and swept wings.

It remained in production long after the 727 and Trident had been superseded by later airliners. The Tu-154M is the last development in the series and it can carry 180 passengers at 590 mph (950 km/h) over a range of 2425 miles (3900 km).

Although over 500 Tu-154s were delivered to Aeroflot, only twenty-nine remain in service with the Russian airline today. Nevertheless, the Tu-154 remains the backbone of the fleets operated by the many new airlines formed in the FSU.

Vickers Viscount

The Viscount, powered by four Rolls-Royce Dart engines, has earned a special place in the history of air transport as the first successful turboprop airliner. Introduced into airline service in 1953, the Viscount quickly attracted orders from many other carriers then operating piston-engined airliners.

Faster, quieter, and more comfortable than its contemporaries, the Viscount became Britain's most successful airliner, with over 700 examples built. Few remain in service today, however, although the Viscount seems assured of a future as a freighter carrying mail in the United Kingdom. For this, British World Airlines operates a fleet of eight Viscount 800s – the stretched model which could accommodate seventy-one passengers.

The later versions of the Viscount cruised at 350 mph (563 km/h) and had a range of 1760 miles (2830 km).

Vickers Vanguard

The Vanguard is much bigger than the Viscount but otherwise similar in layout. Powered by four Rolls-Royce Tyne turboprops, the Vanguard could accommodate up to 139 passengers but it failed to achieve anything like the sales figures of its smaller forebear. This is because the jet era had begun and even comfortable turboprop airliners could not compete with the new faster models.

Introduced in 1961, the Vanguard did not remain in front-line passenger service for long, most operators preferring to use it as a freighter. Thus, it became known as the Merchantman, and the few that remain in service today are operated by such carriers as Hunting Cargo Airlines.

The Vanguard can cruise at 425 mph (685 km/h) and has a range of 1830 miles (2945 km).

Yakovlev Yak-42

Carrying up to 120 passengers, the Yak-42 is the second trijet to be designed by the company. The smaller and earlier Yak-40 could accommodate only thirty-three passengers, however, although over 700 were built.

While the Yak-40 was designed to serve remote communities – if necessary operating from grass runways – the more conventional Yak-42 was intended to replace the Tu-134 on shorter routes.

The Yak-42 entered service in 1980 and development of the design continues today, with 'Westernized' variants planned as a means of addressing export markets. The stretched Yak-42M can seat up to 165 passengers, and this version has a range 1150 miles (1850 km) cruising at 515 mph (830 km/h).

Lockheed Martin F-117A Stealth Fighter

Military Aircraft

Aermacchi MB 339

The latest evolution of a highly successful Italian advanced jet trainer design, the MB 339 has been exported to several countries, in addition to meeting the needs of the Italian Air Force.

The MB 339 was based on the MB 326 which first flew in 1957 and from which it differs mainly in having a stepped cockpit. This enables the instructor to see over the head of the pupil seated in the front of the tandem cockpit – a design feature of most modern jet trainers.

Like the earlier MB 326, however, the 339 can also function as a ground-attack aircraft, carrying bombs, rockets, or machine-gun pods beneath the wings. The MB 339 is powered by a single Rolls-Royce Viper engine which gives it a top speed of 558 mph (900 km/h).

Alenia G-222

Powered by two General Electric T64 turboprops, the G-222 is a high-wing tactical transport aircraft. It can accommodate up to forty-four troops but can also carry light trucks, artillery, or other items of defence equipment.

First deliveries to the Italian Air Force began in 1975, and export orders were received from several countries. Until the early 1990s, however, the production total had not reached three figures, but an order from the United States Air Force gave a boost to the G-222.

Teamed with Lockheed Martin, Alenia may develop a G-222J, employing the same engine and six-bladed propeller combination which are features of the new C-130J transport aircraft.

Bell UH-1

Founder of the 'Huey' family of helicopters, the Bell Model 204 was originally designated HU-1 in US Army service, hence the nickname which has stuck despite the later UH-1 designation.

The Model 204 grew into many other derivatives and, over a period of some twenty years, its gross weight increased almost threefold. It is estimated that around 12,000 Hueys remain in service with air forces around the world. There is no doubt that many will still be flying well into the next century.

The Bell 214ST (*main picture*) is the biggest 'stretch' of the Huey, carrying up to eighteen passengers in a commercial derivative.

British Aerospace VC-10

Originally built by Vickers as a passenger airliner, the VC-10 has found a new life as a tanker/transport. Converted to its military role by British Aerospace, the VC-10 differs little from its original airliner appearance, only a refuelling probe and hose drum units beneath the wings and fuselage indicating its new function.

Both Standard and Super VC-10s are to be seen in RAF colours, the latter being distinguished by its longer fuselage. A total of nine ex-British Airways' VC-10s have been converted by British Aerospace, and the larger of the tankers can carry 176,350 lb (80,000 kg) of fuel.

In its heyday, the Super VC-10 could carry up to 187 passengers over a 7128 mile (11,470 km) range.

British Aerospace Nimrod

First flown in 1968, the Nimrod is based on the Comet airliner. The shape of the original aircraft has been substantially altered, however, by the addition of an unpressurized pannier which extends almost the entire length of the lower fuselage.

The Nimrod is the only jet maritime patrol aircraft but by no means the only one to have been developed from an airliner. Over the years, the Nimrod has been further developed by the installation of improved electronic equipment, but its distinctive shape remains much the same as the original.

The Nimrod has a low-level patrol speed of 230 mph (370 km/h) and it can remain in the air for twelve hours, although inflight refuelling can extend the patrol time if required.

British Aerospace Jaguar

Developed as a joint venture by France and Britain, the Jaguar was the product of SEPECAT – a company formed by BAC and Breguet. Neither company exists today, and British Aerospace took the lead in seeking export orders for this tactical support aircraft.

Powered by two Rolls-Royce/Turbomeca Adour engines, the Jaguar was originally intended to have an advanced trainer role but most of the 402 aircraft ordered for the French Air Force and the RAF are single-seat versions.

All had been delivered by the end of 1981, although some export orders were received. Indeed, the Jaguar may be considered an underrated aircraft but it performed well in the Gulf War and will remain in service well into the next century.

The Jaguar has a maximum speed of 1056 mph (1699 km/h) and may often be seen flying as low as 250 ft during exercises over northern England and Scotland.

British Aerospace Harrier

Introduced into service in 1969, the Harrier is the world's first V/STOL fighter. Vertical/Short Take Off and Landing is an ability normally associated only with helicopters but the Harrier makes use of a jet reaction control system together with four exhaust nozzles.

Powered by a single Rolls-Royce Pegasus engine, the Harrier has been designed to operate from any suitable hide without need of a runway. Development of the Harrier was encouraged by the US Marine Corps which took delivery of its first in 1971.

Employed by the Royal Navy with great success during the Falklands War, the Sea Harrier (*pictured*) is one of several developments which have changed the appearance of the aircraft in detailed respects.

British Aerospace Bulldog

The Bulldog originated in 1969 as a military development of the Beagle Pup two-seat trainer. When the manufacturer went bankrupt, however, production was taken over by Scottish Aviation which, in turn, became part of British Aerospace.

A low-wing aircraft powered by a single 200 hp Lycoming engine, the Bulldog is a fully aerobatic plane which remains in service with the RAF and with the Swedish Air Force. Although the Bulldog still flies with some forces, it is to be retired from the RAF inventory, and it is likely that some of these will be acquired by private owners.

British Aerospace Hawk

The Hawk was designed to replace the Gnat advanced trainer in service with the RAF in the 1970s. A low-wing design powered by a single Rolls-Royce/Turbomeca Adour turbofan, the Hawk has become one of the most successful of British military aircraft.

Although ordered for several air forces after it was selected by the RAF, the Hawk received a major boost when it won a competition to supply the US Navy.

Capable of flying at 625 mph (1000 km/h), the Hawk is usually flown at rather slower speeds in the hands of students.

A single-seat fighter version of the Hawk has been developed but not selected by the RAF. Nevertheless, the Hawk will certainly remain in UK service well into the next century.

British Aerospace Tornado

Strictly, this should be called the Panavia Tornado because it is the product of Deutsche Aerospace and Alenia as well as British Aerospace. Designed to replace several different types of combat aircraft, the Tornado is unusual in having a swing wing. This has the advantage of allowing the pilot to land and take off relatively slowly with the wings moved forward, but to fly at over 1450 mph (2335 km/h) when they are fully swept back.

Although used primarily as a strike aircraft, an interceptor version of the Tornado was also supplied to the RAF. Intended to approach its targets at very low heights, the Tornado may be glimpsed practising this art over more remote parts of the British Isles.

Boeing AWACS

More properly known as the E-3 Sentry, the AWACS (Airborne Warning And Control System) is easily recognized by the very large saucer-shaped rotordome mounted above the rear fuselage. Based on the Boeing 707 airframe, the AWACS has been supplied to the RAF as well as to the United States Air Force, NATO, and other air forces.

The AWACS entered service with the USAF in 1978, initially tasked with aiding America's air defences. In subsequent years, however, examples have played a key defence role in Europe, Asia, and the Middle East. The AWACS can fly for eleven hours without refuelling and it has a maximum speed of 530 mph (853 km/h). It normally carries a crew of seventeen to control and monitor the complex surveillance equipment.

Boeing B-52

Development of the B-52 began in the late 1940s, and the first prototype flew in 1952. Powered by eight engines (which are apt to trail black smoke on take-off), the B-52 is a remarkable bomber which has remained in front-line service with the United States Air Force far longer than originally anticipated.

Steadily developed over the years, later examples of the B-52 were fitted with more powerful engines, and the bomber has been adapted to carry a wide variety of weapons. The B-52 has a maximum speed of 630 mph (1014 km/h) and it was used with success in the Vietnam War and in the more recent Gulf War.

A giant by any measure, the B-52 may well still be in service in the next century. Its successors, the very different B-1 and B-2, are smaller and faster.

Boeing Chinook

Essentially a larger and more powerful version of the earlier CH-46, the first Chinook entered US Army service in 1962. Since that time, the Chinook has undergone many refinements but has changed little in appearance. A tandem-rotor, medium-transport helicopter, the CH-47 Chinook has a large rear door but also carries slung loads.

Over 1200 examples have been supplied to armed forces in many countries, but the civil version – the Model 234 – has been less successful and few remain in service.

In its military guise, the Chinook can carry up to fifty-five troops and has a maximum speed of 185 mph (298 km/h).

Dassault Atlantic

The Atlantic was originally designed in France by Breguet but launched as a multinational NATO programme. This maritime patrol aircraft was supplied for service only in France, Germany, the Netherlands, and Italy, however. Pakistan later acquired some used models from the French Navy.

A twin-turboprop-powered aircraft, the Atlantic cruises at 345 mph (556 km/h) and has a maximum range of 5180 miles (8340 km). A total of eighty-seven 'first-generation' Atlantics was built but a French Navy requirement for a replacement led to the development of the Atlantic 2 which Dassault has produced.

Externally similar to the original model, the Atlantic 2 is fitted with a completely new suite of electronic equipment.

Dassault Alpha Jet

Work on the Alpha Jet began in 1969 when France and Germany announced a requirement for an advanced trainer that could also function as a ground-attack aircraft. A compact, twin-jet with a shoulder wing and tandem seating, the Alpha Jet sold well in export markets and some were produced under licence in Egypt.

While France continues to operate the Alpha Jet, Germany has retired its own fleet which was largely devoted to the ground-attack, rather than the advanced trainer, role. Second-hand examples have been supplied to other air forces – Portugal, for example.

Originally produced by Dassault-Breguet and Dornier, today only the French company is seeking new orders, although none has been built for several years. The Alpha Jet is flown by the French Air Force aerobatic team which occasionally visits Britain.

English Electric Canberra

It is remarkable that some fifty years after the first flight of the Canberra, some examples remain in service today. A twin-jet light bomber, the Canberra was developed into many variants covering some twenty-seven different marks.

Supplied to eleven air forces around the world, a total of 1352 Canberras was built, including licence-produced models in Australia and the United States. In Britain, where 901 examples were produced, responsibility for the Canberra now rests with British Aerospace.

The Canberra has a maximum speed of 517 mph (827 km/h) and a range of 805 miles (1295 km), carrying a bomb-load. It can climb at 3400 ft (1035 m) per minute.

Eurocopter Gazelle

The Gazelle was designed by Aerospatiale to meet a French Army requirement for a light helicopter, for which Britain also had a similar need. So Westland became a partner on the programme in 1967.

A classic in its own time, the Gazelle remains in production today and is in service in many countries. Some were built under licence in the former Yugoslavia, and more than 1500 have been produced. There is no doubt that the Gazelle will remain in service into the twenty-first century.

The current model is powered by a single Astazou 14M turboshaft, and the Gazelle can carry five people including the pilot. Alternatively, weapons such as anti-tank missiles or rockets can be carried.

Fairchild A-10

Officially named Thunderbolt II, the A-10 has been dubbed the 'Warthog' because beauty is not one of its virtues. A low-wing design, powered by two engines mounted on the rear of the fuselage, the A-10 has a twin fin and rudder configuration.

A single-seat close-support/anti-tank aircraft, the A-10 is fitted with a 30 mm Gatling-type cannon and carries up to seven tons of weapons beneath the wings and fuselage. The pilot is protected against light- and medium-calibre weapons by a 'bathtub' made of titanium, and the A-10 itself can survive several hits.

The A-10 is an agile aircraft which was introduced into service in 1974 but, though threatened with retirement several times, its unique capabilities have kept it in front-line service.

Lockheed Martin C-130 Hercules

The first Hercules flew in 1954 and it has since become one of the most remark-able of military transport aircraft. Powered by four Allison T56 turboprop engines, the Hercules has a high wing mounted on a pressurized fuselage which is produced in standard and 'stretched' versions.

Capable of carrying vehicles and other large items of equipment, the Hercules has a rear ramp that can be opened in flight so that supplies can be delivered by parachute. Although the C-130 has a range of 2487 miles (4002 km), it can land and take off from rough airstrips.

Over 2000 Hercules have been produced, and the RAF is one of the largest users outside the United States.

Lockheed Martin C-5B

The C-5A Galaxy was designed by Lockheed in the late 1960s to meet a United States Air Force requirement for a very large strategic transport aircraft. Boeing's entry in the design competition was not selected but went on to become the 747, while the C-5A became the world's largest aircraft.

The Antonov An-225 is the world's largest aircraft today but the C-5 remains the backbone of the USAF's large transport fleet. Adding to the original eighty-one aircraft, a further fifty C-5Bs were produced during the 1980s, but they are identical in appearance.

The C-5B can carry 270 soldiers on its lower deck, but the aircraft is primarily a freighter which can accommodate such loads as two battle tanks or sixteen trucks. It has a range of 3434 miles (5526 km).

Lockheed Martin C-141 StarLifter

The C-141 was developed to enable the United States to deploy troops and equipment quickly to almost any part of the world. A four jet with a high wing and a T-tail, the C-141 has clam-shell rear doors to allow straight-in loading.

The ramp can be lowered for in-flight air drops, while side doors can be used by paratroops. First delivered in 1964, a total of 285 C-141s was produced but many have been rebuilt with a 23 ft (7.1 m) fuselage extension. This enables the stretched C-141 to accommodate thirteen standard pallets instead of the previous ten.

Carrying a maximum payload, the C-141 has a range of some 4000 miles (6450 km).

Lockheed Martin P-3 Orion

In 1957, the United States Navy issued a requirement for a maritime patrol and ASW (anti-submarine warfare) aircraft, and suggested that a development of an aircraft already in production would be preferred. At that time Lockheed was manufacturing the Electra airliner and, although only 170 were built, over 640 of its maritime patrol development have been produced to date.

A low-wing design powered by four turboprops, the Orion has been supplied to the air forces and navies of many countries. During a routine patrol, two of the four engines are often shut down to conserve fuel and, operated in this way, the Orion has an endurance of over 17 hours.

Lockheed Martin F-16 Fighting Falcon

Developed in the 1970s by General Dynamics to meet a USAF requirement for a lightweight fighter, the F-16 has since been supplied to the air forces of many countries. Indeed, the F-16 has been produced under licence in several countries, and it forms the basis of fighters developed in Japan and South Korea.

Over 3500 F-16s have been produced but, when General Dynamics decided to withdraw from the defence business, the programme was taken over by Lockheed Martin. There is no doubt, however, that the F-16 will remain in service well into the twenty-first century, as deliveries continue and more countries seek to buy it.

The cropped delta wings, which blend into the fuselage, give the F-16 a modern appearance which does not seem to date.

Lockheed Martin F-104 Starfighter

Although the F-104 made its first flight in 1954, it remains a remarkable fighter that seems impossible to fly on its tiny wings with a span of only 21 ft 11 in (6.68 m). The F-104 was designed to be superior to anything that the Soviet Air Force could field, and the single-engined Starfighter can achieve a maximum speed of 1300 mph (2092 km/h).

Despite its very small wing, the F-104 can reach a height of 55,000 ft (16,764 m) but few remain in service, because more recent fighters, such as the F-16, are much more adaptable. Neither speed nor height are such crucial factors today, as most air battles are fought at lower altitudes, while modern air-to-air missiles can attack an unseen enemy over the horizon.

Lockheed Martin U-2

At the height of the Cold War, it became the custom to send 'spy planes' over Soviet territory to check on the deployment of its forces. Development of the MiG-15, however, enabled the Soviet Air Force to intercept high-flying B-47 reconnaissance planes.

So, in the mid-1950s the U-2 was developed by Lockheed's 'Skunk Works' to provide an aircraft capable of flying at heights beyond the reach of either fighter or missile defences.

Powered by one jet engine and controlled by a single pilot, the U-2 has a very high aspect-ratio wing much like that of a glider. This enabled the aircraft to reach great heights but the later TR-1 derivative operates at an altitude of over 70,000 ft (21,335 m).

Lockheed Martin F-117A

The F-117A is the first of a new generation of 'stealth' combat aircraft designed to be difficult to detect by radar or any other sensor. This accounts for the strange shape of the F-117A which is designed to reflect radar energy away from an originating transmitter.

Comprising a series of flat surfaces, the wing blends with the fuselage, while all doors, panels, and the cockpit frame have serrated edges to suppress radar reflection. The 1991 Gulf War provided the opportunity to test design theory in practice, and the F-117A succeeded in bombing its targets undetected by ground defences.

The F-117A is powered by two turbofans without reheat and is controlled by a crew of one.

MiG-21

Developed by the Mikoyan and Gurevich design bureau, the MiG-21 first flew in 1955 and the fighter entered service three years later. Powered by a single engine, the MiG-21 has a small delta wing and it can achieve a speed of 1285 mph (2070 km/h).

About 10,000 MiG-21s have been built, including some under licence in India and former Czechoslovakia, while China based its F-8 on the Russian fighter. Many MiG-21s remain in service today and some are being modernized by the installation of Western equipment.

At least twenty-nine countries were supplied with MiG-21s but many have been retired because of increasing maintenance costs.

MiG-29

A contemporary of the F-15 to which it bears some resemblance, the MiG-29 was designed to succeed the MiG-21 and other early combat aircraft. The wing of the MiG-29 blends with the fuselage in a way reminiscent of the F-16 but, unlike the American fighter, it is powered by two engines and has a twin fin and rudder.

Indeed, the MiG-29 has done much to overcome the reputation of Soviet aircraft for poor quality and inferior performance by providing remarkable displays of agility at international air shows. The 'python' manoeuvre in which the MiG-29 flies slowly with its nose raised to a high angle, before pitching down under precise control, has become a popular 'party trick' at air displays.

McDonnell Douglas F-4 Phantom II

Although not the prettiest of fighters, the Phantom is undoubtedly one of the most successful of its period. Making its first flight in 1958, the Phantom has a low-cranked wing, is powered by two J79 engines, and has a crew of two.

Soon recognized to be a fine all-round combat aircraft, the Phantom saw service with the air forces of eleven nations. Although many have been retired, it is still operational in several countries.

The RAF and the Royal Navy acquired the Phantom but the only examples likely to be seen in Britain are those that remain in service with the German Air Force as reconnaissance aircraft.

McDonnell Douglas F-15 Eagle

Said to be the only Western fighter capable of catching the Mach 3 MiG-25, the F-15 was for long a vital United States Air Force contribution to the defence of Europe. The F-15 has also been supplied to the air forces of Israel, Japan, and Saudi Arabia, although most of the more than 1000 produced, have been for the USAF.

Powered by two engines, the F-15 has twin fins and a general layout not unlike that of the MiG-29 and Sukhoi Su-27. Operated by a crew of two, the F-15 is an air superiority fighter which also has a powerful ground-attack capability. Although still built under licence in Japan, production in the United States is tailing off.

McDonnell Douglas F/A-18A Hornet

Developed from the Northrop YF-17 which lost out in the competition held in 1974 to supply the United States Air Force with a lightweight fighter, the F/A-18A has since become a highly successful combat aircraft. While the USAF preferred the single-engined F-16, the US Navy saw the twin-engined YF-17 to be the basis for its lightweight multi-mission requirement.

By 1978, McDonnell Douglas developed the design into the larger F/A-18 which has won export orders from several countries. More than 1000 have been built, and development of the F/A-18 into B, C/D, and the larger E/F models will ensure continued production into the next century.

Most F/A-18s have been supplied as single-seat fighter/attack aircraft, but two-seat versions are also built to meet a need for a trainer that also has a combat capability.

McDonnell Douglas AH-64A Apache

Originally designed and produced by Hughes to meet a United States Army requirement for an advanced attack helicopter, the YAH-64 beat the Bell entry before ownership of the programme passed to McDonnell Douglas.

The twin-engined Apache is no beauty but is a remarkably agile helicopter which can carry a variety of missiles and rockets in addition to the 30 mm chain gun mounted beneath the forward fuselage. It is operated by a crew of two seated in tandem, with the co-pilot/gunner in the front and the pilot on an elevated seat behind.

The Apache proved to be a devastating attack helicopter during the Gulf War and the helicopter has secured orders from several countries, including Britain's Army Air Corps. It is being produced by Westland under licence and will become an increasingly familiar sight.

McDonnell Douglas C-17

A long-range heavy lift transport, the C-17 is capable of delivering its cargo to airstrips with 'minimal' runways. Indeed, the C-17 is required to combine the load-carrying capability of the C-5 with the STOL performance of the C-130.

Like most military freighters, the C-17 has a high wing and a fat body to accommodate vehicles, helicopters, or other large items. Powered by four jet engines, the C-17 has a range of 2765 miles (4445 km) carrying a full load into a 3000 ft (915 m) landing strip.

Recently introduced into service, the C-17 will be seen increasingly in the Britain at one of the United States Air Force bases.

Northrop Grumman F-5

Over 3000 of the F-5 family had been built when production ended in 1987. Designed by Northrop as a lightweight fighter, the F-5 first flew in 1959 but over 1500 remain in service. Indeed, the F-5 is the subject of several modernization programmes which will ensure that it will remain in service well into the twenty-first century.

Although the United States Air Force still operates the broadly similar T-38 supersonic advanced trainer, almost all of the F-5 fighters were supplied to foreign air forces.

Powered by two General Electric J85 turbojets, the F-5E/F (the last versions) can fly at 1083 mph (1743 km/h). Two-seat trainers have been produced but the basic F-5 has a crew of one.

Northrop Grumman B-2

Described as 'a low observable strategic penetration bomber', the B-2 is arguably the strangest sight to be seen in the skies over Britain. A flying wing blended into the fuselage, the B-2 incorporates the latest 'stealth' technology and has no vertical tail surfaces.

It is hard to imagine a greater contrast to the elderly B-52 which the B-2 is designed to supplant, but the B-2 represents the new generation of combat aircraft that are expected to avoid enemy defences by being 'invisible', at least on radar screens.

The B-2 has an un-refuelled range of 7255 miles (11,675 km) and it can fly as high as 50,000 ft (15,240 m).

Saab JAS 39 Gripen

The single-seat Gripen is an advanced combat aircraft from a company which is noted for innovation in fighter design. Of all-composite construction, the Gripen has a delta wing and canards – all-moving foreplanes located above the engine intakes.

Although a two-seat trainer version has been produced to ease conversion to the fly-by-wire fighter, most operational versions are single-seaters. At the press of a button, the role of the Gripen can be switched from interceptor, to that of a ground-attack or reconnaissance aircraft.

Saab has teamed with British Aerospace to promote the Gripen in export markets, and examples are certain to be seen in Britain.

Shorts Tucano

The original Tucano was designed in Brazil by Embraer but, when this turbo-prop-powered trainer was selected by the RAF to replace its Jet Provosts, Shorts was licensed to produce the 130 required. The RAF version differs from the standard model in being powered by a Garrett TPE331 engine in place of the PT6A turboprop fitted to all other examples.

Although some Shorts Tucanos were exported, the aircraft is no longer in production in the United Kingdom. Development of the Tucano continues in Brazil, however, and production into four figures is expected.

A versatile aircraft which can double as a ground-attack fighter, the Tucano has been selected by air forces all over the world.

Sikorsky UH-60A Black Hawk

First flown in 1974, the Black Hawk is a worthy successor to the famous 'Huey'. Although not yet produced in such numbers as its forebear, the Black Hawk has nevertheless found customers all over the world, and it has been supplied in many versions to US forces.

Powered by two General Electric T700 turboshafts, the Black Hawk has a range of 373 miles (600 km) and a maximum speed of 184 mph (296 km/h). The Black Hawk can carry up to fourteen troops but it can also mount a variety of weapons, and has been adapted to operate from warships in an anti-submarine warfare (ASW) role.

Although a commercial variant has been produced, most customers use them in military or paramilitary roles.

Sikorsky CH-53

Known variously as the 'Jolly Green Giant', Sea Dragon, and Super Stallion, the CH-53 was originally developed to meet a US Marine Corps need. Utilizing the dynamic system developed for the S-64 Skycrane, the CH-53 has a large fuselage into which equipment can be loaded via a ramp at the rear.

Examples which entered service in 1964 were powered by two engines driving a single six-bladed main rotor. Three engines power the later versions, however, including the Super Stallion and Sea Dragon. The later models can carry up to fifty-five troops but the helicopter is also used as a mine sweeper, towing a hydrofoil 'sledge' over the water.

The CH-53 is in service with the forces of several countries in addition to those of the United States.

Transall C-160

The Transport Alliance (Transall) was formed in 1959 to produce a military transport for the air forces of France and Germany. A twin turboprop-powered, high-wing design with a rear loading ramp, the C-160 follows the classic military transport configuration.

Initially, a total of 179 was produced and examples were exported to Turkey and South Africa. A French requirement for additional C-160s, however, resulted in the production of a second batch which incorporated detailed improvements.

The C-160 has a range of 3166 miles (5095 km) carrying an 17,640 lb (8000 kg) payload, although the aircraft can carry double that amount over a shorter range.

A few of the second-series C-160s were sold to a commercial operator, but only military examples are seen in Britain.

Westland Wessex

Built under licence from Sikorsky, the Wessex entered service with the Royal Navy in 1960. Later adopted by the RAF and exported to several countries, the Wessex remains in service today, although numbers are diminishing.

Originally acquired for anti-submarine tasks by the Royal Navy, the Wessex has since been used as a commando assault transport, for search and rescue, and as a VIP transport with the Queen's Flight. It has a maximum speed of 133 mph (214 km/h) and a range of 390 miles (630 km).

Although Sikorsky built some S-58s for commercial operators, few remain in service and examples to be seen in Britain are likely to be military.

Westland Lynx

Produced in two basic versions, the Lynx is a fast multi-role helicopter which originates from an Anglo-French agreement concluded in 1968. While Westland was given design leadership for the Lynx, its French partner Aerospatiale led on the design of the Puma and Gazelle. All three were produced as a joint programme by the two companies.

Although the Lynx has been supplied in quantity to the British Army and the Royal Navy, however, it is the naval variant that has done well in export markets. Indeed, the Navy Lynx has become a market leader, while Battlefield Lynx and other developments of the Army variant, have failed to secure overseas orders.

Steadily upgraded with more powerful engines, advanced rotor blades, and a comprehensive electronics suite, Navy Lynx is to be replaced by the Royal Navy with the Merlin but will be around for many more years.

Westland Sea King

In 1969, Westland produced the first Sea King built under licence from Sikorsky. Although based on the S-61 passenger transport helicopter, however, Westland produced only the military Sea King version.

It has been a highly successful helicopter, with Westland continuing to manufacture examples long after Sikorsky closed its production line. The Royal Navy has been Westland's biggest customer but many have been exported, including the 'Commando' tactical transport variant.

The Sea King has been developed for many roles, the most unusual of which is an Airborne Early Warning version equipped with a surveillance radar in an air-pressurized container on a swivel mounting.

Westland EH-101 Merlin

A joint venture with Agusta of Italy, the EH-101 is a three-engined multi-role helicopter which, in Royal Navy service, is called Merlin. Much larger than the Lynx, the Merlin will nevertheless eventually replace it and the Sea King in Royal Navy service.

The EH-101 is also on order for the RAF which will use it as a tactical transport. It has a rear loading ramp and can accommodate up to thirty-five troops or defence equipment. The Heliliner is a commercial variant which can carry thirty passengers and is intended to be a successor to the S-61.

Despite its size, the EH-101 can operate from frigates which previously carried the Lynx or similar helicopters.

Avro Lancaster

Historic Aircraft

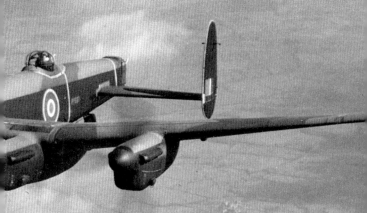

Antonov An-2

More than 17,000 An-2s have been built since the first example flew in 1947. Indeed, it could be described as a piece of flying history because, although it is a biplane, it has remained in production for almost fifty years!

Powered by a single 1000 hp radial piston engine, the An-2 can carry twelve passengers but has been used for many different tasks including crop spraying. The An-2 is capable of operating from grass runways and can get airborne after a run of just 492 ft (150 m), But it has a top speed of only 160 mph (258 km/h).

Most An-2s were built in Poland and some are in use in Britain.

Avro Lancaster

The Lancaster was the most successful of the heavy bombers used by the RAF during World War II. Powered by four Rolls-Royce Merlin engines, the Lancaster grew from an unsuccessful twin-engined bomber called the Manchester. It became a versatile aircraft which carried out many raids that have earned a place in military history.

A total of 7366 Lancasters was built but few remain even in museums. A well-preserved example may be seen at air shows throughout Britain by courtesy of the RAF Historic Flight, however.

Today a single Tornado can deliver as much devastation as a squadron of World War II bombers but, in its time, the Lancaster was the most effective in its class.

Boeing B-17 Flying Fortress

The first B-17 took to the air in July 1935 but the model which equipped many US Army Air Corps' squadrons during World War II was a much improved version. In particular, the B-17E, F, and G had a much-improved defensive armament and a larger fin.

Machine-guns could be fired from seven positions on the Flying Fortress, and this explains the United States policy of carrying out bombing raids by day. Britain preferred to operate its bombers by night so that they would be more difficult to detect and attack.

Some Flying Fortresses have been preserved and one may be seen at air displays in Britain.

Bristol Fighter

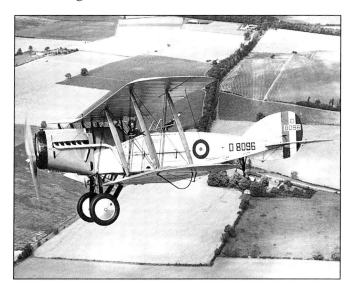

Widely known as the 'Brisfit', the Bristol Fighter saw service in the final two years of World War I and, by its end, some 3800 had been produced. A further 1303 were built before production ended in 1926, however, although only one airworthy example remains in existence. This is owned by the Shuttleworth Collection and can be seen at some of the displays organized each summer at Old Warden Aerodrome in Bedfordshire.

A two-seat army co-operation aircraft, the Bristol Fighter is powered by a remarkably quiet 280 hp Rolls-Royce Falcon engine which gives it a maximum speed of 125 mph (201 km/h). In its later years until 1931, the Brisfit served as a trainer.

Consolidated Catalina

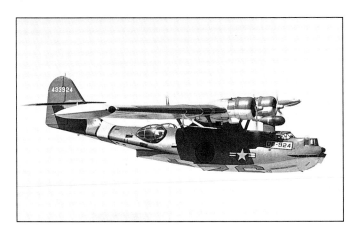

The Catalina entered service with the United States Navy in 1936 but went on to be the most widely used flying boat during World War II. Over 500 Catalinas were built for the RAF alone, and fortunately some examples have survived.

Powered by two Pratt & Whitney Twin Wasp piston engines mounted close together on a high wing, the Catalina has a range of 4000 miles (6436 km) and an endurance of over seventeen hours.

Two large side-blister windows are an unusual feature of the Catalina and, as well as providing a good observation point for the crew, they also housed a machine-gun. Operated as the PBY-5 by the US Navy, the Catalina carried a 2000 lb (868 kg) weapon load.

de Havilland Tiger Moth

In service with the RAF for over fifteen years, the Tiger Moth became one of the world's most famous trainers. A single-engined biplane with tandem seating in open cockpits, the Tiger Moth started its career in 1932 and it was still the RAF's standard elementary trainer in 1947.

Produced in Australia, Canada, and New Zealand as well as in the UK, a total of 8300 Tiger Moths was built. The last biplane to serve with the RAF, the Tiger Moth has a maximum speed of only 109 mph (175 km/h) but is fully aerobatic.

Much sought after by private owners, several Tiger Moths remain on the British civil register.

de Havilland Mosquito

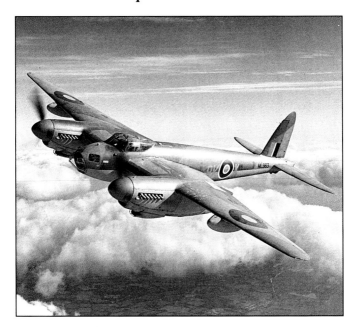

Together with the Spitfire and Lancaster, the Mosquito was generally acknowledged to be one of the most successful aircraft of World War II. The first Mosquito began flight trials in February 1941 but, by July of that year, it was in full production!

Of all-wood construction, the lightweight Mosquito had a maximum speed of 425 mph (683 km/h) and, in its initial reconnaissance and bomber versions, was unarmed. It relied on its speed to avoid enemy fighters and, until 1944, the Mosquito was the fastest aircraft in the RAF.

Including some made in Australia and Canada, a total of 7781 Mosquitoes was built, and the RAF operated them until 1953. A handful has survived and, until it crashed at an air display in 1996, one was seen flying in Britain occasionally.

Douglas DC-3

The most famous of all airliners, the DC-3 entered service in 1934. A low-wing design powered by two Pratt & Whitney Twin Wasp piston engines, the DC-3 is unpressurized and was originally intended to carry twenty-four passengers.

World War II was to establish the DC-3 as a highly versatile transport aircraft known in the United States as the C-47 and named the Dakota by the RAF. A total of 10,655 examples was built in the United States and some more were produced under licence in the Former Soviet Union (FSU).

Although the numbers are declining, both civil and military DC-3s remain in service in many parts of the world. Some in the United Kingdom have been adapted for use in treating oil spills.

Fairey Swordfish

Affectionately known as the 'Stringbag', the Swordfish was one of the most remarkable aircraft of World War II. A single-engined biplane capable of a maximum speed of only 139 mph (223 km/h), the Swordfish continued in Royal Navy service as a torpedo and dive bomber throughout the war.

Operated from aircraft carriers, the Swordfish equipped no less than twenty-five Fleet AirArm squadrons. Despite its slow speed, the Swordfish is highly manoeuvrable and it recorded many achievements during the war, sinking a German submarine at night for the first time.

A flying example is maintained by the Royal Navy and is a welcome visitor to flying displays in Britain.

Hawker Hart

The Hart was one of the most versatile and adaptable biplanes to serve with the RAF. Powered by a single Rolls-Royce Kestrel engine, the two-seat Hart could fly at a maximum speed of 184 mph (296 km/h) and, in 1930, it could outrun the fighters of the day.

Over 500 Harts were built but some were converted to become trainers, while others were purpose-built for this role. The single-seat Fury fighter, (the first RAF fighter to exceed 200 mph (321 km/h), Demon two-seat fighter, and Audax army co-operation aircraft were in many respects identical to the Hart.

It is fitting that a flying example of the Hart should be preserved in the Shuttleworth Collection.

Hawker Hurricane

The first production Hurricane flew in 1937 and, within a year, the RAF had ordered 1000. It has its roots in the Hawker Fury biplane and was developed just in time to play a key role in the Battle of Britain in which it shot down more enemy aircraft than all other defences combined.

Initially mounting eight machine-guns, the Hurricane later carried four 20 mm cannon or could carry two bombs beneath the wings. Powered by a Rolls-Royce Merlin engine, the Hurricane was the first RAF fighter to exceed 300 mph (482 km/h), although it was later outperformed by the Spitfire in this respect.

A total of 12,780 Hurricanes was built in Britain, with a further 1451 manufactured in Canada. Few have survived but the RAF Historic Flight keeps one in flying condition and rumour has it that some have survived in the FSU.

Hawker Hunter

The Hunter entered service with the RAF in 1954 and it says much for its outstanding performance that Switzerland only recently retired its last example. The Hunter remains on the strength of the Zimbabwe Air Force, however, and there is no doubt that airworthy examples are still flying.

Powered by a Rolls-Royce Avon turbojet, the Hunter is a single-seat interceptor, although some two-seat trainers were also produced. Normally armed with four 30 mm cannon, the Hunter can also carry bombs or rockets.

Generally regarded as a superb all-round combat aircraft, a total of 1985 Hunters was produced including some built under licence in Belgium and the Netherlands.

Junkers Ju-52/3m

The prototype of the Ju-52/3m first flew in 1932 and it quickly became a popular airliner, Lufthansa operating over fifty within four years. Developed from a single-engined design, the tri-motor Ju-52 is notable for its corrugated metal skin, if a further distinguishing feature were needed!

Capable of carrying seventeen passengers, the Ju-52 was operated by several airlines but, with Europe preparing for war once again, the Luftwaffe acquired a large number to serve as bombers. During World War II, however, the Ju-52 was used mainly as a transport and for glider-towing.

Approximately 4870 Ju-52s were built and, of the few survivors, one is kept in flying condition by Lufthansa and it visits Britain occasionally.

Messerschmidt Me 109

The low-wing, single-seat Me 109 fighter was first flown in 1935, and some 35,000 had been built by 1955 when the last licence-produced example took to the air in Spain. By then, the original engine was no longer available, so the Rolls-Royce Merlin was used instead.

The airworthy examples of the Me 109 which survive today are almost all Spanish-built but only purists will declare them to be impostors! The Me 109 was used by the Luftwaffe as a fighter and attack aircraft during World War II but some saw service with the Swiss Air Force.

The Me 109 could not fly as fast as the Spitfire, achieving a maximum of 354 mph (569 km/h), but it was highly manoeuvrable and robust.

Miles Messenger

The single-engined, low-wing Miles Messenger was used during World War II as the personal transport of Field Marshal Montgomery. First flown in 1942, the Messenger has a maximum speed of only 135 mph (217 km/h) but its agility and slow-flying capability enables it to be flown into short airstrips.

Large Fowler flaps, together with a three fin and rudder configuration, contribute to the excellent performance of the Messenger as an air-observation and communications aircraft.

After the war, the Messenger remained in production but only sixty had been built when the line was closed in 1948. At least one remains airworthy, however, and may be seen at air shows in Britain.

North American Harvard

Known as the T-6 Texan in the United States, the Harvard is a two-seat trainer powered by a single Pratt & Whitney Wasp engine. The high speed of the direct-drive propeller results in a distinctive rasping noise which aids recognition but is not heard by the occupants.

The Harvard entered service with the RAF in 1938, the same year in which the T-6 began to replace earlier trainers in the US Army Air Corps. In addition to the United States, some thirty-three countries acquired Harvards, and South Africa is only now in the process of replacing them!

The airworthy Harvards which remain in Britain are in the hands of private owners but are often seen at air displays.

North American Mustang

The Mustang was designed as a low-wing, single-seat fighter-bomber, and later versions were powered by American-built Merlin engines. As the P-51, the Mustang was used extensively by the US Army Air Corps as an escort fighter for bomber groups, but the Mustang later became a useful ground-attack aircraft.

A total of 1670 was supplied to the RAF, the Mustang's 442 mph (711 km/h) maximum speed proving to be invaluable in combating the V-1 flying bombs during 1944. After World War II, many Mustangs were acquired by private owners for use as racers in the United States, but at least one is still flying in Britain and is often seen at flying displays.

Vickers Supermarine Spitfire

The legendary Spitfire was developed as a private venture and, although it took some time to interest the government of the day, its outstanding performance finally persuaded the Air Ministry to place an order in 1936.

First deliveries to the RAF began in 1938 and, together with the Hurricane, the Spitfire is credited with winning the Battle of Britain. Like the Hurricane, the Spitfire is powered by a single Rolls-Royce Merlin and a total of 18,298 was built. A further 2053 Griffon-engined Spitfires were produced, however. Several Spitfires have survived including some now kept in flying condition by the RAF Historic Flight and seen occasionally at air displays in Britain.

Index